MW00779223

THE FIRE AND THE TALE

MERIDIAN

Crossing Aesthetics

Werner Hamacher

Editor

THE FIRE AND THE TALE

Giorgio Agamben

Translated by Lorenzo Chiesa

STANFORD UNIVERSITY PRESS

STANFORD, CALIFORNIA

Stanford University Press
Stanford, California

English translation © 2017 by the Board of Trustees of the
Leland Stanford Junior University. All rights reserved.

The Fire and the Tale was originally published in Italian in 2014
under the title *Il fuoco e il racconto* © 2014, Nottetempo.

No part of this book may be reproduced or transmitted in any form or by
any means, electronic or mechanical, including photocopying and record-
ing, or in any information storage or retrieval system without the prior
written permission of Stanford University Press.

Printed in the United States of America on acid-free,
archival-quality paper

Library of Congress Cataloging-in-Publication Data

Names: Agamben, Giorgio, 1942– author.
Title: The fire and the tale / Giorgio Agamben ;
translated by Lorenzo Chiesa.
Other titles: Fuoco e il racconto. English | Meridian (Stanford, Calif.)
Description: Stanford, California : Stanford University Press, 2017. |
Series: Meridian: crossing aesthetics | "Originally published in Italian
in 2014 under the title Il fuoco e il racconto." |
Includes bibliographical references.
Identifiers: LCCN 2016039696 | ISBN 9780804798716 (cloth : alk. paper)
| ISBN 9781503601642 (pbk. : alk. paper) | ISBN 9781503601659 (e-book)
Subjects: LCSH: Literature—Aesthetics. | Literature—Philosophy.
Classification: LCC PN45 .A25813 2017 | DDC 801/.93—dc23
LC record available at https://lccn.loc.gov/2016039696

Contents

The Fire and the Tale

At the end of his book on Jewish mysticism Gershom Scholem tells the following story, which he learned from Yosef Agnon:

> When the Baal Schem, the founder of Hasidism, had a difficult task before him, he would go to a certain place in the woods, light a fire and meditate in prayer; and what he had set out to perform was done. When a generation later, the Maggid of Meseritz was faced with the same task, he would go to the same place in the woods, and say: "We can no longer light a fire, but we can pray." And everything happened according to his will. When another generation had passed, Rabbi Moshe Leib of Sassov was faced with the same task, [and] he would go to the same place in the woods, and say: "We can no longer light a fire, nor do we know the secret meditations belonging to the prayers, but we know the place in the woods, and that can be sufficient." And sufficient it was. But when another generation had passed and Rabbi Israel of Rishin was called upon to perform the task, he sat down in his golden chair, in his castle, and said: "We

cannot light the fire, we cannot speak the prayers, we do not know the place, but we can tell the story of all this." And, once again, this was sufficient.[1]

It is possible to read this anecdote as an allegory of literature. In the course of its history, humanity moves further and further away from the sources of mystery and, little by little, loses the memory of what tradition taught it about the fire, the place, and the formula—but of all this men can still tell the story. What remains of mystery is literature, and "that can be sufficient," the rabbi comments with a smile. The meaning of this "can be sufficient" is, however, not easy to grasp, and perhaps the destiny of literature depends precisely on how we understand it. If we simply understand it in the sense that the loss of the fire, the place, and the formula is somehow progress and that the result of this progress—secularization—is the liberation of the tale from its mythical sources and the establishment of literature—now autonomous and adult—in a separate sphere—that is, culture—then that "can be sufficient" really becomes enigmatic. It can be sufficient—but to what? Is it credible that we can be satisfied with a tale that is no longer in relation with the fire?

After all, by saying "we can tell the story *of all this*," the rabbi claimed exactly the opposite. "All this" means loss and forgetting, and what the tale tells is indeed the story of the loss of the fire, the place, and the prayer. Each tale—all literature—is, in this sense, a memory of the loss of the fire.

Literary historiography has by now accepted that the novel derives from mystery. Kerényi and, after him, Reinhold Merkelbach have demonstrated the existence of a genetic link between pagan mysteries and the ancient novel, of which Apuleius's *Metamorphosis* offers us a particularly convincing document (here the protagonist, who has been transformed into an ass, finds in the end salvation by means of a literal mystery initiation). This nexus is manifested by the fact that, exactly like in mysteries, we see in novels an individual life that is connected with a divine or in any case superhuman element, whereby the events, episodes, and vicissitudes of a human existence acquire a meaning that overcomes them and constitutes them as a mystery. Just like the initiated—attending in the dimness of Eleusis the mimicked or danced evocation of the abduction of Kore by Hades and her annual reappearance on Earth in spring—penetrated mystery and found in it the hope of having his life saved, so the reader, following the series of situations and events that the novel weaves pitifully or ferociously around its character, somehow participates in his destiny and, at any rate, introduces his own existence to the sphere of mystery.

Yet this mystery is separated from any mythical content and religious perspective, and hence can be somehow desperate, as happens with Isabel Archer in Henry James's novel or with Anna Karenina. This mystery can even show a life that has entirely lost its mystery, as in Emma Bovary's story. In any case, if what is at stake is a novel, there will always be an initiation, however miserable and confined to nothing other than life as such and its squandering. It belongs to the nature of the novel to be at the same time loss and commemoration of the mystery, disarray and remembrance of the formula and the place. If the novel forgets the memory of its ambiguous relation with the mystery, as always more often happens today, or if, cancelling any trace of the precarious and uncertain Eleusinian salvation, it claims to have no need for the formula, or worse, consumes the mystery in a host of private facts, then the very form of the novel is lost together with the memory of the fire.

The element in which the mystery is dispersed and lost is history [*storia*]. We need to think again and again about the fact that the same term designates both the chronological progress of human events and what literature relates, both the historical gesture of the researcher and that of the narrator. We can access the mystery only through a story [*storia*], yet (or maybe we

should say, "in fact") history [*storia*] is that in which
the mystery has put out or hidden its fires.[2]

In a letter of 1937, starting from his personal experience as a scholar of the *qabbalah*, Scholem tried to
reflect on the implications of the nexus that knots
two at least apparently contradictory elements such
as mystical truth and historical investigation. He
intended to write "not the history, but the metaphysics
of the Cabala"; however, he soon realized that it was
not possible to access the mystical kernel of tradition
(*qabbalah* means "tradition") without going through
the "wall of history":

> The mountain [this is how Scholem refers to mystical
> truth] needs no key at all; only the misty wall of history,
> which hangs around it, must be penetrated. To penetrate
> it was the task I set for myself. Will I get stuck in the
> mist, will I suffer, so to speak, a "professorial death"?
> But the necessity of historical criticism and critical his-
> tory cannot be replaced by anything else, even where it
> demands sacrifices. Certainly, history may seem to be a
> fundamental illusion, but an illusion without which, in
> temporal reality, no insight into the essence of things is
> possible. That mystical totality of truth, whose exis-
> tence disappears precisely when being projected onto
> historical time, can become visible for today's man in a
> primary and pure way only in the legitimate discipline
> of commentary and the strange mirror of philological
> critique. Today, as at the very beginning, my work lives
> in this paradox, in the hope of being truly addressed

from within the mountain, of that most inconspicuous, that smallest possible fluctuation of history, which causes truth to break forth from the illusions of "development."[3]

The task that Scholem defines as paradoxical is, following the teaching of his friend and mentor Walter Benjamin, that of transforming philology into a mystical discipline. As in every mystical experience, it is for this reason necessary to throw oneself wholeheartedly into the obscurity and mist of philological inquiry, with its melancholy archives and gloomy documents, with its unreadable manuscripts and abstruse glosses. There is undoubtedly a very strong risk of losing one's way in philological practice, of not remaining focused on the mystical element that we wish to achieve— because of the *coniunctivitis professoria* that this practice involves. But like the Grail that was lost in history, the researcher must lose himself in his philological *quête*, because this very bewilderment is the only guarantee of the seriousness of a method, which is to the same extent a mystical experience.

If investigating history and telling a story are, in all truth, the same gesture, then the writer himself faces a paradoxical task. He will have to intransigently believe only in literature—that is, in the loss of the fire. He will have to forget himself in the story that he weaves around his characters, and yet, even if only at this price, he will have to know how to discern at the end of this oblivion the fragments of black light that come from the lost mystery.

"Precarious" refers to what is obtained by means of a prayer (*praex*, a verbal request, as different from *quaestio*, a request that is made with all available means, even violent ones) and is, for this, fragile and adventurous. Literature is itself adventurous and precarious, if it wishes to preserve the right relation with the mystery. Like the initiated at Eleusis, the writer proceeds in darkness and dimness, on a path suspended between infernal and celestial gods, between oblivion and remembrance. There is, however, a thread, a sort of probe sent toward the mystery, which allows him to measure his distance from the fire at each turn. This probe is language, and it is on language that the intervals and breaks that separate the tale from the fire are implacably marked as wounds. Literary genres are the sores that the oblivion of the mystery has inflicted on language: tragedy and elegy, hymn and comedy are nothing other than the ways in which language cries for its lost relation with the fire. Today, writers do not seem to notice these wounds. They walk as if blind and deaf over the abyss of their language and do not hear the lament that cries from the bottom; they believe they are using language as a neutral instrument and do not perceive the resentful babbling that calls for the formula and the place, that demands accountability and vengeance. To write means to contemplate language. And those who do not see and love their language, those who are unable to spell out its tenuous elegy or perceive its murmured hymn, are not writers.

The fire and the tale, the mystery and the story are the two indispensable elements of literature. But in what way can one of the elements, whose presence is the irrefutable proof of the loss of the other, bear witness to this absence, exorcising its shadow and memory? Where there is the tale, the fire is out; where there is the mystery, there cannot be the story.

Dante has condensed in a single verse the situation of the artist faced with this impossible task: "the artist / who for the habit of art has a hand that trembles" (*Paradise* 13.77–78). The language of the writer—like the gesture of the artist—is a field of polar tensions, whose extremes are style and manner. "The habit of art" is the style, the perfect possession of one's means, in which the absence of the fire is peremptorily assumed, because the work contains everything and can lack nothing. There is no mystery, and there never was one, because it is entirely exposed here and now and forever. But, in this imperious gesture, a trembling is at times produced, something like an intimate vacillation, in which style suddenly overflows, colors fade, words stutter, and matter clots and spills over. This trembling is the manner that, in the deposition of the habit, attests once again to the absence and the excess of the fire. And in any good writer, in any artist, there is always a manner that takes its distance from the style, a style that disappropriates itself as manner. In this way the mystery undoes and loosens the plot of the story; the fire creases and consumes the page of the tale.

Henry James once told how his novels originated. At the beginning there is only what he calls an *image en disponibilité*, the isolated vision of a man or a woman still devoid of any determination. That is, they present themselves as "available," so that the author may weave around them the fatal intrigue of situations, relations, encounters, and episodes that "will make them come out in the most appropriate way," to make them become, in the end, what they are, the "complication that they are more likely to produce and feel." That is: being characters.

The story that, in this way, page after page, while it narrates their successes and failures, their salvation and damnation, exhibits and reveals them, is also the plot that seals them into a destiny, constitutes their lives as a *mysterion*. It makes them "come out" only to enclose them in a story. In the end, the image is no longer "available," has lost its mystery, and can only perish.

Something similar also happens in the lives of men. Without a doubt, in its inexorable course, existence—which initially seemed so available, so rich with possibilities—little by little loses its mystery, one by one puts out its fires. It is, in the end, only a story, insignificant and disenchanted like any other. Until one day—perhaps not the last, but the second to last—existence finds again for an instant its enchantment and all of a sudden atones for its disappointment. What has lost its mystery is now truly and irreparably mysterious, truly and absolutely unavailable. The fire, which can only be told, the mystery, which was integrally violated in a story, now leaves us speechless and shuts itself away forever in an image.

Mysterium Burocraticum

Perhaps there is no better place than the footage of Eichmann's trial in Jerusalem to glimpse the intimate and unmentionable correspondence that unites the mystery of guilt with the mystery of punishment. On the one side, enclosed in his cage of glass, the accused: he seems to catch his breath and feel at home only when he can meticulously enumerate the names of his departments and correct the imprecisions of the prosecution with regard to numbers and acronyms. On the other side, pompously facing him, the prosecutor: in the same determined way, he threatens the accused with his inexhaustible pile of documents, each evoked through its bureaucratic monogram.

Beyond the grotesque element that frames the dialogue of the tragedy of which the two are the protagonists, there is truly an enigma here: office IV-B4, where Eichmann worked in Berlin, and Beth Hamish-

path, Jerusalem's House of Justice in which the trial
is held, duly correspond to each other, and somehow
are the same place, just as Hauser, the prosecutor who
accuses Eichmann, is his exact double in the mystery that unites them. And both seem to be aware of
this. If, as has been said, a trial is a "mystery," this is
indeed one that, unappeased, links together in a dense
network of gestures, acts, and words guilt and punishment.

Yet what is at stake here is not, like in pagan mysteries,
a mystery of salvation, however precarious; nor is
it—like in Mass, which Honorius of Autun defines
as a "trial that takes place between God and his
people"—a mystery of atonement. The *mysterion* that
is held in the House of Justice knows neither salvation
nor atonement, since, independently of its outcome,
the trial is in itself the punishment. The sentence can
only prolong and sanction it, and acquittal can in no
way invalidate it, since it is only the acknowledgment
of a *non liquet*, of the insufficiency of judgment.
Eichmann, his ineffable lawyer Servatius, the gloomy
Hauser, the judges, each in his own lugubrious attire,
are nothing other than the quibbling officiants of the
only mystery that is still accessible to modern man:
this is not so much the mystery of evil, in its banality
or profundity (in evil we never have mystery, only the

semblance of mystery), but the mystery of guilt and punishment, or rather of their undecipherable nexus, which we call Judgment.

It now seems certain that Eichmann was an ordinary man. We should therefore not be surprised that this police officer, whom the prosecution tries in every possible way to present as a ruthless killer, was an exemplary father and a generally well-intentioned citizen. The fact is that the very mind of an ordinary man represents today an unexplainable conundrum for ethics. When Dostoyevsky and Nietzsche realized that God is dead, they believed they had to draw the conclusion that man would become a monster and an abomination, and that nothing and nobody could hold him back from committing the most nefarious crimes. This prophecy turned out to be unsubstantiated— and yet somehow correct. No doubt, there are, from time to time, apparently decent kids who gun down their classmates in a school in Colorado, and, in the outskirts of big cities, petty criminals and infamous assassins. But, as has always been the case, and perhaps to an even greater extent, they are an exception and not the rule. The ordinary man survived God without too much difficulty and, rather, is today unexpectedly respectful of law and social conventions, instinctively inclined to abide by them, and, at least with respect to others, eager to invoke their implementation. It is as if the prophecy according to which "if God is dead, then everything is permitted" did not concern him in any way: he continues to live reasonably even without the comfort of religion and endures with resignation a life that has lost its metaphysical sense, a life about which he does not, after all, seem to have any illusions.

There is, in this sense, a heroism of the ordinary man. It is a sort of everyday mystical practice; like the mystic who, at the moment of entering the "obscure night," tarnishes and deposes one after the other the powers of the senses (night of hearing, of sight, of touch . . .) and of the soul (night of memory, of the intellect and the will), the modern citizen dismisses, along with these powers and almost distractedly, all the characteristics and attributes that defined human existence and made it livable. For this he does not need the *pathos* that distinguished the two figures of the human after the death of God: Dostoyevsky's underground man and Nietzsche's superman. Whatever the view of these two prophets, living *etsi Deus non daretur*[1] is, for the ordinary man, the most obvious circumstance, even if he was certainly not given the opportunity to choose it. The *routine* of metropolitan existence, with its endless de-subjectivizing apparatuses and

its cheap and unwitting ecstasies, is, if need be,
perfectly sufficient.

It is to this approximate being, this hero without
assignable task, that is allotted the hardest ordeal: the
mysterium burocraticum of guilt and punishment. The
latter was thought up for him, and in him alone it
finds its ceremonial accomplishment. Like Eichmann,
the ordinary man experiences a ferocious moment
of glory during the trial; at any rate, it is the only
moment in which the opacity of his existence acquires
a meaning that appears to transcend him. But exactly
like in capitalist religion according to Benjamin,
it is a mystery without salvation or redemption, in
which guilt and punishment have been integrally
incorporated into human existence; the mystery can
therefore not disclose any beyond to human existence
nor confer upon it any comprehensible sense. There is
the mystery, with its impenetrable gestures, its events
and arcane formulas: but it is so flattened onto human
life that it perfectly coincides with it and does not let
transpire any hint of another place or possible justice.

It is because of the awareness—or, rather, the
premonition—of this atrocious immanence that Franz
Stangl, the commander of the Treblinka extermina-
tion camp, can continue to declare his innocence
until the end and, at the same time, concede that his

guilt—he was then guilty—was simply to have found himself where he was: "My conscience is clear with what I have done . . . but I was there."

In Latin the bond [*vincolo*] that ties guilt to punishment is called *nexus*. *Nectere* means "to tie," and *nexus* is the knot, the *vinculum* with which the one who utters a ritual formula is bound. The Twelve Tables express this "nexus" sanctioning that *cum nexum faciet mancipiumque, uti lingua nuncupassit, ita ius esto*, "when [someone] makes a bond and takes the thing in his hand, as language has said, so let the law be." Pronouncing the formula is equivalent to realizing the law, and the one who in this way says the *ius* is obliged, that is, is bound to what he has said, in the sense that he will have to answer for his noncompliance (that is, he will be guilty). *Nuncupare* literally means "taking the name," *nomen capere*, just as *mancipium* refers to the act of taking in one's hand (*manu capere*) the thing to be sold or bought. Those who have taken on the name and have pronounced the established word cannot retract it and let it come to nothing: they are bound to their word and will have to keep it.

On close inspection this means that what unites guilt and punishment is nothing other than language. Having pronounced the formula is something irrevocable, just like, for the living being who, one day (we do not know how or why), began to speak, having spoken, having entered into language is irrecusable. That is, the mystery of guilt and of punishment is the mystery of language. The sentence that man is serving, the trial against him that has been ongoing for forty thousand years—that is, since he began to speak—is nothing other than speech itself. "Taking the name," naming oneself and things, means being able to know and master oneself and things; but it also means submitting to the powers of guilt and law. For this, the ultimate decree that can be read between the lines of all codes and all earthly laws reads: "Language is the punishment. All things must enter into it and perish in it according to the extent of their guilt."

language as law

The *mysterium burocraticum* is, then, the extreme commemoration of anthropogenesis, of the immemorial act through which the living being, by speaking, has become a man, has been bound to language. For this, it concerns both the ordinary man and the poet, both the wise man and the ignorant, both the victim and the executioner. And, for this, the trial is always under way, because man does not stop becoming a man and remaining inhuman, entering and exiting humanity. That is, he does not stop accusing himself and claiming to be innocent, declaring, like Eichmann, that he is ready to hang himself in public and, yet, that he is innocent before the law. And until man is able to get to the bottom of his mystery—the mystery of language and of guilt, that is, in all truth, of his being and not yet being human, of his being and no longer being an animal—the Judgment, in which he is at the same time the judge and the accused, will not stop being deferred, will continuously repeat its *non liquet.*

Parable and Kingdom

In the Gospels, Jesus often speaks in parables, so
often, in fact, that the Italian verb *parlare*, "to speak,"
unknown to classical Latin, derives from this habit
of the Lord: *parabolare*, that is, to speak like Jesus,
who "did not speak to them without a parable" (*choris
paraboles ouden elalei*, Matt. 13:34). But the eminent
place of the parable is the "Kingdom speech" (*logos
tes basileias*). In Matthew 13:3–52, eight parables (the
Sower, the Tares, the Mustard Seed, the Leaven, the
Hidden Treasure, the Merchant and the Pearl, the
Dragnet, the Scribe) follow one another to explain to
the Apostles and the crowd (*ochlos*, the "mass") how
to understand the Kingdom of heaven. *Kingdom* and
parable are in such close and constant proximity that
a theologian could write that "the *basileia* is expressed
in the parable as a parable" and that "Jesus's parables
express the Kingdom of God as a parable."[1]

The parable has the form of a simile. "The Kingdom of heaven is similar [*homoia*] to a mustard seed . . ."; "the Kingdom of heaven resembles [*homoiothe*] a man who sows . . ." (in Mark 4:26: "the Kingdom of God is thus like [*outos . . . os*] a man who scatters seed . . ."). That is, the parable establishes a similarity between the Kingdom and something that is here and now on Earth. This means that the experience of the Kingdom goes through the perception of a similarity and that without the perception of this similarity it is impossible for men to understand the Kingdom. From this follows its affinity with the parable: parables express the Kingdom of heaven as a parable because such a Kingdom first of all means the event and perception of a similarity: with the leaven that a woman mixes into three measures of flour; with the hidden treasure that a man finds in a field; with a net thrown into the sea that gathers all kinds of fish; and, above all, with the act of the sower.

The reasons Jesus gives for speaking in parables are themselves enigmatic. In Matthew 13:10–17, when asked by the Apostles why he speaks to the crowds in parables, Jesus answers:

> Because the knowledge of the secrets of the kingdom of heaven has been given to you, but not to them. Whoever has will be given more, and they will have an abun-

dance. Whoever does not have, even what they have
will be taken from them. This is why I speak to them in
parables: because though seeing they do not see; though
hearing they do not hear or understand.

Admittedly, the Apostles have themselves not understood, given that, soon after, Jesus has to explain to
them the parable of the sower.

In Luke 8:9–16 the reasons Jesus gives seem different; after repeating that the Apostles were given the
knowledge of the secrets of the Kingdom which others
receive in parables "so that though seeing, they may
not see, though hearing they may not understand,"
in total contradiction Jesus adds that "no one lights a
lamp and hides it in a jar or puts it under a bed" and
that "there is nothing hidden that will not be dis-
closed, nothing concealed that will not be known or
brought out into the open." According to a rhetorical
model that was common in Antiquity, parables are a
discourse ciphered to prevent those who should not
understand it from understanding it; yet, at the same
time, they fully display the mystery. It is likely that the
explanations Jesus gives for his speaking in parables
are themselves a parable, which works as an introduction to the parable of the sower ("Hear ye therefore the
parable of the sower . . .").

The correspondence between the Kingdom and the world, which parables present as a similarity, is also expressed by Jesus as a proximity in the stereotypical formula "the Kingdom of heaven has come near [*eggiken*]" (Matt. 3:2 and 10:7; Mark 1:15; Luke 10:9). *Eggys*, "close," from which the verb *eggizo* derives, arguably comes from a term that means "hand": that is, the proximity of the Kingdom is not only of a temporal order—as one would expect of an eschatological event that coincides with the end of times—but also and especially of a spatial order: it is, literally, "close at hand." This means that the Kingdom, which is the ultimate thing par excellence, is essentially "close" to penultimate things, which it resembles in parables. The similarity of the Kingdom is also a proximity; the Ultimate is, at the same time, close and similar.

The special proximity of the Kingdom is also attested to by the fact that it is expressed in the Gospels by a peculiar confusion of past and future. So much so that, in the Beatitudes, while those who mourn *will* be comforted, the meek *will* inherit the Earth, those who hunger and thirst for righteousness *will* be filled, and the pure in heart *will* see God, the pure in spirit and those who are persecuted because of righteousness *are* blessed "for theirs is the Kingdom of heaven." It is as if

the phrase "Kingdom of heaven" required the present
tense, even where we would rather expect a future
tense. In Luke 11:12 Jesus says without doubt that
"now the Kingdom of heaven has come" (the aorist
efthasen expresses the exact occurrence of an event);
yet in Mark 14:25 we find a present tense although
the context would undoubtedly require a future tense
("Truly I tell you I *will not drink* again [*pio*, aorist
subjunctive] from the fruit of the wine until that day
when I *drink* it new [*pino kainon*] in the Kingdom of
heaven"). It is perhaps in Luke 17:20–21 that this real
threshold of indifference between tenses is expressed
in the clearest way. On being asked by the Pharisees:
"When does the Kingdom of God come [*erchetai*]?"
Jesus answers: "The coming of the Kingdom of God
is not something that can be observed, nor will people
say, 'Here it is,' or 'There it is,' because the Kingdom
of God is close at your hand" (this is the meaning of
entos ymon, not "in your midst"). The presence—it
is a matter of presence—of the Kingdom has the
form of a proximity. (The invocation in the prayer of
Matthew 6:10, "Your Kingdom come [*eltheto*]," does
not contradict at all this apparent confusion of tenses:
as Benveniste reminds us, the imperative does not
actually have a temporal character.)

Precisely because the presence of the Kingdom has the form of a proximity, it finds its most congruous expression in parables. And it is this special link between parable and Kingdom that is somehow thematized in the parable of the sower. Explaining it (Matt. 13:18–23), Jesus establishes a correspondence between the seed and the word of the Kingdom (*logos tes basileias*; in Mark 4:15 it is clearly stated that "the farmer sows the *logos*"). The seed sown along the path refers to "those who hear the message about the Kingdom and do not understand it"; the seed fallen on rocky ground means those who hear the word, but are erratic and "when trouble and persecution comes because of the word, they quickly fall away"; the seed falling among the thorns is someone who hears the word, but remains unfruitful, since he lets the word be choked by the worries of this life; "but the seed falling on good soil refers to someone who hears the word and understands it."

Thus, the parable does not immediately concern the Kingdom but the "word of the Kingdom," that is, the very words that Jesus has just uttered. The parable of the sower is therefore a parable about parables, in which access to the Kingdom is equated with understanding the parable.

The fact that there is a correspondence between the understanding of parables and the Kingdom was the most ingenious discovery made by Origen, the founder of modern hermeneutics—the Church has always considered him as the best among the good and, at the same time, the worst among the wicked. As he himself tells us, Origen heard a parable from a Jew according to which

> inspired Scripture taken as a whole was on account of its obscurity like many locked-up rooms in one house. Before each room a key was placed, but not the one belonging to it; and the keys were so dispersed all round the rooms, not fitting the locks of the several rooms before which they were placed.[2]

The key of David "that openeth, and none shall shut, and that shutteth, and none openeth" is what allows the interpretation of Scriptures and, at the same time, gives access to the Kingdom.[3] According to Origen, it is for this that, addressing the custodians of the law who obstruct the right interpretation of the Scriptures, Jesus said, "Woe to you teachers of the law and Pharisees, you hypocrites! You shut the door of the Kingdom of heaven and do not let enter those who are trying to" (Matt. 23:13).

Yet it is in his commentary on the parable of the scribe "instructed unto the Kingdom of heaven," the last of a long list of similes about the Kingdom found in Matthew, that Origen clearly enunciates his discovery. The scribe in question in the parable is the one who,

> having received elementary knowledge through the literal meaning [*dia tou grammatos*, "through the letter"] of the Scriptures, ascends to the spiritual meaning [*epi ta pneumatika*], which is called the Kingdom of the heavens. And according as each thought is attained, and grasped abstractly and proved by example and absolute demonstration, can one understand the kingdom of heaven, so that he who abounds in knowledge free from error is in the kingdom of the multitude of what are here represented as "heavens."[4]

To understand the sense of the parable means to open the doors of the Kingdom; but, given that the keys have been swapped, this very understanding is the most difficult thing.

One of Hölderlin's late hymns, which has reached us in four different versions and whose title—*Patmos*—certainly refers to a Christological context, is dedicated to the experience of the Kingdom's proximity and to the parable of the sower. That the problem in question concerns the proximity of the Kingdom of God and, at the same time, the difficulty of accessing it is made clear at the beginning of the first draft: "God is near / Yet hard to seize." At stake in this difficulty is nothing less than salvation: "Where there is danger / The rescue grows as well."

The darkness (*Finstern*) evoked shortly after is not without relation to the Scriptures, for the poet can ask for "wings, and the truest minds / To voyage over and then again return more faithful." Only this New Testament context can explain the sudden evocation of the parable of the sower. Those who were close to God and lived in his memory have now lost the sense of his word:

> Perplexed and no longer understood
> One another
>
> . . . And even the Highest turns aside his
> Countenance, so that nothing
> Immortal can be seen either
> In heaven or upon the green earth.

"What meaning must we take from all of this?" asks the distraught poet. With perfect coherence the answer refers to the parable of the "word of the Kingdom," which is lost and no longer understood:

> It is the cast of the sower, as he seizes
> Wheat with his shovel
> Throwing it in the clean air.

But here the interpretation of the parable undergoes a peculiar reversal: that the seed is lost and the word of the Kingdom remains unfruitful is, according to the poet, not something evil:

> The chaff falls to his feet, but
> The grain emerges in the end.
> It's not bad if some of it gets lost,
> Or if the sounds of His living speech
> Fade away.

And, against tradition, what needs to be attended to is the literal sense, not the spiritual one:

> But what our Father
> Who reigns over everything wants most
> Is that the established Word be
> Caringly attended, and that
> Which endures be construed well.

The word of the Kingdom is doomed to be lost and remain unappreciated if it were not for its literality. And this is something good, for the song comes precisely from this care for the letter: "German song must accord with this." No longer understanding the word of the Kingdom is a poetic condition.

On Parables (*Von den Gleichnissen*) is the title of a posthumous fragment by Kafka, published by Max Brod in 1931. Apparently, as the title seems to suggest, it is a parable about parables. The meaning of the short dialogue that takes place between two speakers (no mention is made of a third, who declaims the first text) is, however, precisely the opposite, namely, that the parable on parables is no longer a parable:

> Many complain that the words of the wise are always merely parables and of no use in daily life, which is the only life we have. When the sage says "Go over," he does not mean that we should cross over to some actual place, which we could do anyhow if the labor were worth it; he means some fabulous yonder, something unknown to us, something too that he cannot designate more closely [*näher*], and therefore cannot help us here in the very least. All these parables really set out to merely say that the incomprehensible is incomprehensible, and we know that already. But the cares we have to struggle with every day: that is a different matter.

An anonymous voice (*einer*) suggests the solution to the problem: "Why such reluctance? If you only followed the parables you yourselves would become parables and with that rid yourself of all your daily cares." Yet the objection made by the second speaker—"I bet that is also a parable"—seems insurmountable: even becoming a parable and exiting reality are, according to all evidence, only a parable, something the first speaker has no difficulty in conceding ("You have won"). It is only at this point that he can clarify the meaning of his suggestion and unexpectedly turn his defeat into a victory. When the second lightheartedly comments: "But unfortunately only in parable," he answers without any irony: "No, in reality: in parable you have lost."

Those who carry on maintaining the distinction between reality and parable have not understood the meaning of the parable. Becoming parable means comprehending that there is no longer any difference between the word of the Kingdom and the Kingdom, between discourse and reality. For this, the second speaker, who insists on believing that the exit from reality is still a parable, can only lose. For those who turn themselves into word [*parola*] and parable [*parabola*]—the etymological derivation shows here all its truth—the Kingdom is so close that it can be seized without "going over."

According to the tradition of medieval hermeneutics, the Scriptures have four senses (which one of the authors of the Zohar assimilates to the four rivers of Eden and the four consonants of the word *Pardes*, "heaven"): the literal or historical; the allegoric; the tropologic or moral; and the anagogic or mystical. The last sense—as is implicit in its name (*anagoge* means movement upward)—is not a sense among others, but indicates the passage to another dimension (in Nicholas of Lyra's formula, it indicates *quo tendas*, "where you have to go"). A common mistake here is to treat the four senses as different, but substantially

homogeneous, as if, for instance, the literal sense
referred to a given place or person and the anagogic
to another place or person. Against this equivocation,
which gave rise to the vacuous idea of an infinite
interpretation, Origen does not tire of reminding us:

> One should not think that historical events are types of
> other historical events, and that bodily things are types
> of other bodily things, but that bodily things are types
> of spiritual things, and that historical events are types of
> intelligible events.

The literal sense and the mystical one are not
two separate senses but homologous: the mystical
sense is nothing other than the raising of the letter
beyond its logical sense, its own transfiguration into
comprehension—that is, the cessation of any further
sense. Understanding the letter, becoming parable
means letting the Kingdom come into it. The parable
speaks "as if we were not the Kingdom," but precisely
and only in this way it opens the door of the Kingdom
for us.

The parable on the "word of the Kingdom" is then a
parable on language, that is, on what still and always
remains for us to understand—our being speakers.
Comprehending our dwelling in language does
not mean knowing the sense of words, with all its

ambiguities and subtleties. It rather means noticing
that what is at stake in language is the proximity
of the Kingdom, its similarity to the world—the
Kingdom is so close and so similar that we struggle
to acknowledge it. For its proximity is a demand
and its similarity an apostrophe, which we need to
fulfill. The word was given to us as parable, not to
distance us from things but to keep them close, even
closer—as when we recognize a similarity in a face; as
when a hand touches us lightly. To speak in parables
[*parabolare*] is simply to speak [*parlare*]: *Marana tha*,
"Come, Lord!"

What Is the Act of Creation?

The title "What Is the Act of Creation?" evokes
that of a lecture given by Gilles Deleuze in Paris in
March 1987. Deleuze defined the act of creation as an
"act of resistance." Resistance to death, first of all, but
also resistance to the paradigm of information media,
through which power [*potere*] is exercised in what he
calls "control societies"—to distinguish them from the
disciplinary societies analyzed by Foucault. Each act of
creation resists something—for example, Deleuze says,
Bach's music is an act of resistance against the separation of the sacred from the profane.

Deleuze does not define what "to resist" means
and appears to give this term the current meaning of
opposing a force or an external threat. In the conversation on the word *resistance* in the *Abécédaire*, he adds,
with reference to the work of art, that to resist always
means to free a potentiality [*potenza*] of life that was

imprisoned or offended; however, even here a real
definition of the act of creation as an act of resistance
is missing.

After many years spent reading, writing, and studying,
it happens at times that we understand what is
our special way—if there is one—of proceeding in
thought and research. In my case, it is a matter of
perceiving what Feuerbach called the "capacity for
development" contained in the work of the authors I
love. The genuinely philosophical element contained
by a work—be it an artistic, scientific, or theoretical
work—is its capacity to be developed; something that
has remained—or has willingly been left—unspoken
and that needs to be found and seized. Why does this
search for the element liable to be developed fascinate
me? Because if we follow this methodological principle
all the way, we inevitably end up at a point where it is
not possible to distinguish between what is ours and
what belongs to the author we are reading. Reaching
this impersonal zone of indifference, in which every
proper name, every copyright, and every claim to
originality fades away, fills me with joy.

   I will therefore try to question what has remained
unspoken in the Deleuzian idea of the act of creation
as an act of resistance, and, in this way, I will endeavor

to continue and carry on—obviously, with full responsibility—the thought of an author I love.

I have to begin by saying that I am rather uneasy about the use of the term *creation* with respect to artistic practices, which is unfortunately very common today. While I was investigating the genealogy of this use, I discovered to my surprise that architects are partly responsible for it. When medieval theologians had to explain the creation of the world, they drew on an example that had already been given by the Stoics. Thomas Aquinas writes that just as a house preexists in the mind of the architect, so, too, did God create the world looking at the model he had in his mind. Naturally, Thomas still distinguished between *creare ex nihilo*, which defined divine creation, and *facere de materia*, which defined human deeds. At any rate, the comparison between the act of the architect and that of God already contains the seed of the transposition of the paradigm of creation onto the activity of the artist.

For this, I rather prefer to speak of the poetic act, and although I will continue to avail myself of the term *creation* for convenience, I would like it to be understood without any emphasis, in the simple sense of *poiein*, "to produce."

Understanding resistance only as an opposition to an external force does not seem to me to be sufficient for a comprehension of the act of creation. In a planned preface to *Philosophische Bemerkungen*, Wittgenstein observed how having to resist the pressure and friction that an age of barbarity opposes to creation ends up dispersing and fragmenting the forces of an individual (his age was for him one of barbarity; ours is certainly such for us). This is so true that, in the *Abécédaire*, Deleuze felt obliged to specify that the act of creation constitutively has to do with the liberation of a potentiality.

I think, however, that the potentiality liberated by the act of creation must be a potentiality that is internal to the very act, just like the act of resistance must be internal to it. Only in this way does the relation between resistance and creation and that between creation and potentiality become intelligible.[1]

In Western philosophy the concept of potentiality has a long history, which we can date back to Aristotle. Aristotle opposes potentiality (*dynamis*) to actuality (*energeia*)—and, at the same time, he links them; this opposition, which marks both his metaphysics and his physics, was bequeathed first to philosophy and then to medieval and modern science. It is through this opposition that Aristotle explains what we call acts of creation, which for him coincided more soberly with the exercise of the *technai* (the arts in the most general sense of the term). The examples he gives to illustrate the passage from potentiality to actuality are in this sense significant: the architect (*oikodomos*), the cithara player, the sculptor, but also the grammarian and, in general, anyone who has a knowledge or a technique. That is to say, the potentiality of which Aristotle speaks in book 9 of the *Metaphysics* and in book 2 of *De Anima* is not a generic potentiality, according to which we say that a child can become an architect or a sculptor, but that which belongs to those who have already acquired the corresponding art or knowledge. Aristotle calls this potentiality *hexis*, from *echo*, "to have": habit, that is, the possession of a capacity or ability.

The one who possesses—or has the habit of—a potentiality can both actualize it and not actualize it. Aristotle's brilliant, even if apparently obvious, thesis is that potentiality is essentially defined by the possibility of its non-implementation. The architect is powerful [*potente*] insofar as he is capable of not building; potentiality is the suspension of the act. (This is well known in politics, where there is even a figure, the so-called provocateur, who has in fact the task of obliging those who have power [*potere*] to exercise it, or actualize it.) It is in this way that, in the *Metaphysics*, Aristotle responds to the theses of the Megarians, who claimed, not without good reason, that potentiality exists only in the act (*energei mono dynastai, otan me energei ou dynastai, Met.* 1046b29– 30). Aristotle objects that, if this were the case, we could not consider an architect to be an architect when he is not building or call "doctor" a doctor who is not exercising his art. What is at stake is, then, the way of being of potentiality, which exists in the form of *hexis*, of mastery over a privation. There is a form or presence of what is not in act, and potentiality is this privative presence. As Aristotle states without reservation in an extraordinary passage of his *Physics*: "*steresis*, privation, is like a form" (*eidos ti, Phys.* 193b19–20).

Following his characteristic gesture, Aristotle pushes this thesis to the extreme, to the point at which it seems to almost turn into an aporia. From the fact that potentiality is defined by the possibility of its non-implementation, he infers that there is a constitutive co-belonging of potentiality and impotentiality.[2] In *Met.* 1046a29–32 he writes: "Impotentiality [*adynamia*] is a privation contrary to potentiality [*dynamis*]. Every potentiality is the impotentiality of the same and with respect to the same (of which it is the potentiality) [*tou autou kai kata to auto pasa dynamis adynamia*]." *Adynamia*, "impotentiality," does not mean here the absence of any potentiality, but the potentiality-not-to (pass to the act), *dynamis me energein*. That is to say, this thesis defines the specific ambivalence of every human potentiality, which, in its original structure, always maintains a relation with its own privation and is always—and with reference to the same thing—the potentiality to be and not to be, to do and not to do. For Aristotle it is this relation that constitutes the essence of potentiality. The living being, who exists in the mode of potentiality, is capable of his own impotentiality, and only in this way does he possess his own potentiality. He can be and do because he preserves a relation with his own not-being and not-doing. In potentiality, sensation is constitutively anesthesia; thought is non-thought; work [*opera*] is inoperativity.

If we recall that the examples of the potentiality-not-to [*potenza-di-non*] are almost always derived from the field of human techniques and knowledge (grammar, music, architecture, medicine), we can then say that man is the living being that exists eminently in the dimension of potentiality, of the power-to and the power-not-to [*dimensione della potenza, del potere e del poter-non*]. Every human potentiality is co-originally impotentiality; every power-to-be or -do is, for man, constitutively in relation with its own privation.

If we go back to our question about the act of creation, this means that the latter cannot at all be understood, following the current idea, as a simple transit from potentiality to actuality. The artist is not the one who possesses a potentiality to create that, at a certain point, he decides—we do not know how and why—to realize and actualize. If every potentiality is constitutively impotentiality, potentiality-not-to, how can the passage to the act take place? The act of the potentiality to play the piano is certainly, for the pianist, the performance of a piano piece; but what happens to the potentiality not to play when he starts to play? How is a potentiality not to play realized?

We can now understand in a new way the relation between creation and resistance Deleuze spoke about. In each act of creation there is something that resists and opposes expression. "To resist," which comes from the Latin *sisto*, etymologically means "to stop, to hold down," or "to stop oneself." This power [*potere*] that withholds and stops potentiality [*potenza*] in its movement toward the act is impotentiality [*impotenza*], the potentiality-not-to [*potenza-di-non*].

That is, potentiality is an ambiguous being that not only is both capable of something and of its opposite, but contains in itself an intimate and irreducible resistance.

If this is the case, we then need to look at the act of creation as a field of forces stretched between potentiality and impotentiality, being capable to act and to resist and being capable not to act and not to resist. Man is capable of mastering his potentiality and accessing it only through his impotentiality; but, precisely for this reason, there is in the end no mastery over potentiality, and being a poet means being at the mercy of one's own impotentiality.

Only a potentiality that is capable of both potentiality and impotentiality is then a supreme potentiality. If every potentiality is both potentiality to be and potentiality not to be, the passage to the act can only take place by transferring one's own potentiality-not-to in the act. This means that if the potentiality to play and the potentiality not to play necessarily belong to every pianist, Glenn Gould is, however, the one who is capable of *not* not playing; the one who, directing his potentiality not only to the act but also to his own impotentiality, plays, as it were, with his potentiality not to play. In the face of ability, which simply negates and abandons its potentiality not to play, and talent, which can only play, mastery preserves and implements in the act not its potentiality to play but the potentiality not to play.

Let us now analyze more concretely the action of resistance in the act of creation. Like the inexpressive in Benjamin, which shatters in the work the claim to totality advocated by appearance, resistance acts as a critical instance that slows down the blind and immediate thrust of potentiality toward the act, and, in this way, prevents potentiality from being resolved and integrally exhausted in the act. If creation were only potentiality-to-, which cannot but blindly cross into the act, art would lapse into execution, which proceeds with false confidence toward a complete form, since it has repressed the resistance of the potentiality-not-to. Contrary to a common equivocation, mastery is not formal perfection but quite the opposite: it is the preservation of potentiality in the act, the salvation of imperfection in a perfect form. In the painting of a master or on a page of a great writer, the resistance of the potentiality-not-to is marked in the work as the intimate mannerism present in every masterpiece.

And it is precisely on this being capable-not-to [*poter-non*] that eventually rests every properly critical instance; what an error of taste makes evident is always a lack that is not so much on the level of the

potentiality-to- but on that of the being capable-
not-to. Those who lack taste cannot refrain from
something; tastelessness is always being incapable not
to do something.

What stamps a seal of necessity on the work is thus
precisely what might have not been or might have
been different: its contingency. Here it is not a matter
of the painter's changing his mind, as shown by a
radiograph under the layers of color, nor of the first
drafts or the variants attested to by a manuscript; what
is at stake is, rather, that "light, imperceptible tremble"
in the very immobility of the form, which, according
to Focillon, is the insignia of classical style.

Dante has summarized this amphibious character
of poetic creation in one verse: "the artist / who for
the habit of art has a hand that trembles." From the
perspective we are interested in, the apparent contradiction between habit and hand is not a defect,
but perfectly expresses the twofold structure of every
creative process that is authentic, intimately and
emblematically suspended between two contradictory
urges: thrust and resistance, inspiration and critique.
And this contradiction pervades the entirety of the
poetic act, given that habit already somehow contra-
dicts inspiration, which comes from elsewhere and,
by definition, cannot be mastered in a habit. In this

sense, the resistance of the potentiality-not-to, deactivating the habit, remains faithful to inspiration and almost prevents it from reifying itself in the work: the inspired artist is without work. But the potentiality-not-to cannot be in turn mastered and transformed into an autonomous principle that would end up impeding any work. What is decisive is that the work always results from a dialectic between these two intimately connected principles.

In an important book, Simondon wrote that man is, as it were, a two-phase being, which results from the dialectic between a non-individuated part and an individual and personal part. The pre-individual is not a chronological past that, at a certain point, is realized and resolved in the individual: it coexists with it and remains irreducible to it.

In this perspective, it is possible to think the act of creation as a complicated dialectic between an impersonal element that precedes and overcomes the individual subject and a personal element that obstinately resists it. The impersonal is the potentiality-to-, the genius that drives toward the work and expression; the potentiality-not-to is the reticence that the individual opposes to the impersonal, the character that tenaciously resists expression and imprints it with its mark. The style of a work does not only depend on the impersonal element, that is, the creative potentiality, but also on what resists and almost enters into conflict with it.

However, the potentiality-not-to does not negate potentiality and form, but, through its resistance, somehow exhibits them; similarly, manner is not simply opposed to style, but can, at times, highlight it.

Dante's line is, in this sense, a prophecy that announces Titian's late paintings, as evidenced, for instance, by the *Annunciation*, housed in the church of San Salvador, Venice. When we observe this extraordinary canvas, we cannot but be struck by the way in which, not only in the clouds that stand above the two figures but even on the wings of the angel, color clogs up and, at the same time, is hollowed out in what has for good reason been defined as a crackling magma, where "flesh trembles" and "lights fight the shadows." It is not surprising that Titian signed this work with an unusual formula, *Titianus fecit fecit*: "made it and remade it," that is, almost unmade it. The fact that radiographs revealed under this writing the usual formula *faciebat* does not necessarily mean that we are dealing with a later addition. On the contrary, it is possible that Titian deleted it precisely in order to stress the peculiarity of his work, which, as Ridolfi suggested—possibly referring to an oral tradition that dated back to Titian—those who commissioned it deemed it to be "not reduced to perfection."

From this stance it is possible that the writing one can read on the bottom below the flower pot, *ignis ardens non comburens*—which refers to the episode of the burning bush from the Bible and, according to theologians, symbolizes the virginity of Mary—might have been inserted by Titian precisely to stress the specific character of the act of creation, which burnt on the surface of the canvas without, however, being consumed—a perfect metaphor for a potentiality that is in flames without running out.

For this reason his hand trembles, but this trembling is supreme mastery. What trembles and almost dances in the form is potentiality: *ignis ardens non comburens*.

From here follows the pertinence of the great figures of creation that are found so frequently in Kafka's work, where the great artist is defined precisely by an absolute inability with respect to his art. On the one hand, this is the confession of the great swimmer:

> I have, admittedly, broken a world record. If, however, you were to ask me how I achieved this, I could not answer adequately. Actually, I cannot even swim. I have always wanted to learn, but have never had the opportunity.

On the other hand, we have the extraordinary singer of the mouse people, Josephine, who not only does not know how to sing, but can barely whistle like her fellows do; nonetheless, precisely in this way, "she gets effects which a trained singer would try in vain to achieve among us and which are only produced because her means are so inadequate."

Perhaps not elsewhere than in these figures has the current idea of art as a knowledge or habit been put more radically into question: Josephine sings with her impotentiality to sing, just like the great swimmer swims with his inability to swim.

Bacon's art X

The potentiality-not-to is not another potentiality juxtaposed to the potentiality-to-: it is its inoperativity, what results from the deactivation of the schema potentiality/actuality. In other words, there is an essential link between the potentiality-not-to and inoperativity. Like Josephine, who, thanks to her inability to sing, exposes the whistle all mice are able to emit, which is, in this way, "set free from the fetters of daily life" and shown in its "true essence," the potentiality-not-to, suspending the passage to the act, renders potentiality inoperative and exposes it as such. Being capable not to sing is, first and foremost, a suspension and an exhibition of the potentiality to sing, which is not simply transferred to the act, but

turns onto itself. That is, there is no potentiality not
to sing that precedes the potentiality to sing and that
should thus be annulled for potentiality to be realized
in singing: the potentiality-not-to is a resistance
internal to potentiality, which prevents the latter from
simply being exhausted in the act and pushes it to turn
onto itself, to become *potentia potentiae*, that is, to be
capable of its own impotentiality.

    The works—for instance, *Las Meninas*—that result
from this suspension of potentiality do not simply
represent their object: along with it they present the
potentiality—the art—with which it has been painted.
In the same way, great poetry does not simply say what
it says, but also the fact that it is saying it, the potentiality and the impotentiality to say it. Painting is the
suspension and exposition of the potentiality of the
gaze, just as poetry is the suspension and exposition of
language.

The way in which our tradition has thought
inoperativity is as self-reference, the turning onto itself
of potentiality. In a famous passage of book Lambda
of the *Metaphysics* (1074b15–35), Aristotle states that
"thought [*noesis*, the act of thinking] is the thought
of thought [*noeseos noesis*]." The Aristotelian formula
does not mean that thought takes itself as its object
(if this were the case, we would have—paraphrasing

the terminology of logic—a meta-thought, on the one hand, and an object-thought, a thought that is thought and not thinking, on the other).

As Aristotle suggests, the aporia concerns the very nature of the *nous*, which, in *De Anima*, is defined as a being of potentiality ("it has no other nature but being a potentiality" and "no being is in act before thinking," 429a21–24) and, in the *Metaphysics*, is rather defined as a pure act, a pure *noesis*:

> If it thinks, but thinks something else that dominates it, its essence will not be the act of thinking [*noesis*, thinking thought], but potentiality, and it cannot then be the best thing. . . . If it is not thinking thought, but potentiality, then the continuity of the act of thinking would be wearisome to it.

The aporia is solved if we recall that, in *De Anima*, Aristotle writes that the *nous*, when each of the intelligibles is actualized, "remains in a sense potential . . . and is then capable of thinking itself" (*De Anima*, 429b9–10). While, in the *Metaphysics*, thought thinks itself (i.e., there is a pure act), in *De Anima*, we rather have a potentiality that, insofar as it is capable not to pass to the act, remains free, inoperative, and is thus capable of thinking itself. This is something like a pure potentiality.

It is this inoperative remainder of potentiality that makes possible the thought of thought, the painting of painting, the poetry of poetry.

That is to say, if self-reference implies a constitutive excess of potentiality over any realization in the act, it is then necessary not to forget that thinking self-reference correctly implies, first and foremost, the deactivation and the abandonment of the apparatus subject/object. In Velázquez's or Titian's canvases, painting (the *pictura picta*) is not the object of the subject that paints (of the *pictura pingens*), just like, in Aristotle's *Metaphysics*, thought is not the object of the thinking subject, which would be absurd. On the contrary, the painting of painting means simply that painting (the potentiality of painting, the *pictura pingens*) is exposed and suspended in the act of painting, just like the poetry of poetry means that language is exposed and suspended in the poem.

I realize that the term *inoperativity* comes up time and time again in these reflections on the act of creation. At this stage it is perhaps appropriate for me to try to delineate at least some elements of what I would like to define as a "poetics—or politics—of inoperativity." I have added the term *politics* because the attempt to think the *poiesis*—that is, the deeds of man—in a different way cannot but put into question even the way in which we conceive of politics.

In a passage from the *Nicomachean Ethics* (1097b22–30), Aristotle raises the question of man's work and incidentally suggests the hypothesis that man lacks a specific kind of work, that he is essentially an inoperative being:

> For just as for a flute-player, a sculptor, or any artist [*technites*], and, in general, for all those who have a work [*ergon*] or activity [*praxis*], the good [*tagathon*] and the well [*to eu*] appear to consist of this work, so should it be for man, if he has a work [*ti ergon*]. Or [shall we say that] the carpenter and the tanner have a function and activity, and man [as such] has none? Is he born without a work [*argos*, "inoperative"]?

In this context, *ergon* does not simply mean "work," but rather defines the *energeia*, the activity or being-in-act specific to man. In the same sense, Plato already wondered about what the *ergon*, the specific activity, was—for instance, that of the horse. The question about the work or absence of work of man has therefore a decisive strategic value, since what depends on it is not only the possibility of assigning a specific nature or essence to man, but also, from Aristotle's stance, that of defining his happiness and hence his politics.

Obviously, Aristotle soon leaves aside the hypothesis that man as an animal is essentially *argos*, inoperative, and that no work or vocation can define him.

For my part I would like to encourage you to take this hypothesis seriously and, consequently, to think man as a living being without work. This is by no means an uncommon hypothesis: to the outrage of theologians, politologists, and fundamentalists of any kind, it has repeatedly resurfaced in the history of our culture. I would like to refer to just two of these re-emergences in the twentieth century. The first comes from the field of science, that is, the extraordinary booklet written by Ludwig Bolk, professor of anatomy at the University of Amsterdam, entitled *Das Problem der Menschwerdung* (*The Problem of Anthropogenesis*, 1926). According to Bolk, man does not descend from an adult primate but from a primate fetus that has acquired the ability to reproduce. In other words, man is a monkey cub that has evolved as an autonomous species. This accounts for the fact that, with respect to other living beings, man is and remains a being of potentiality, able to adapt to all environments, all food, and all activities, yet none of these can ever contain or define him.

The second example, this time from the field of arts, is Kazimir Malevich's peculiar pamphlet *Inop-

erativity as the Real Truth of Mankind; against the tradition that sees in labor the realization of man, here inoperativity is affirmed as the "highest form of humanity," of which the white—the ultimate level reached by Suprematism in painting—becomes the most appropriate symbol. Like all attempts at thinking inoperativity, even this text—similarly to his direct precedent, Lafargue's *The Right to Be Lazy*—remains trapped in a negative determination of its own object, since it defines inoperativity only *e contrario* with respect to labor. While for the ancients it was labor— *negotium*—that was defined negatively with respect to contemplative life—*otium*—moderns seem unable to conceive of contemplation, inoperativity, and feast otherwise than as rest or the negation of labor.

Since we are rather trying to define inoperativity in relation to potentiality and the act of creation, it goes without saying that we cannot think it as idleness or inactivity but as a praxis or potentiality of a special kind, which maintains a constitutive relation with its own inoperativity.

In *Ethics*, Spinoza uses a concept that seems to me helpful to understand what we are discussing. He calls *acquiescentia in se ipso*[3] "a joy born of the fact that man contemplates himself and his potentiality to act" (IV, Proposition 52, Demonstration). What does it mean to "contemplate one's own potentiality to act"? What is an inoperativity that consists of contemplating one's own potentiality to act?

I believe it is a matter of, so to speak, an inoperativity internal to the operation itself, a sui generis praxis that, in the work, first and foremost, exposes and contemplates potentiality, a potentiality that does not precede the work, but accompanies it, makes it live, and opens it to possibilities. The life that contemplates its own potentiality to act and not to act becomes inoperative in all its operations, lives only its livableness.

We then understand the essential function that the tradition of Western philosophy has ascribed to contemplative life and inoperativity: the true human praxis is that which, rendering inoperative the specific works and functions of the living being, makes them, so to speak, run around in circles and, in this way, opens them as possibilities. Contemplation and inoperativity are, in this sense, the metaphysical operators of anthropogenesis, which, freeing the living human being from any biological or social destiny and from any predetermined task, make him available for that particular absence of work we are used to calling "politics" and "art." Politics and art are neither tasks nor simply "works": they rather name the dimension in which linguistic and bodily operations—material

and immaterial, biological and social—are deactivated
and contemplated as such.

I hope that at this point what I mean by "poetics
of inoperativity" is somehow clearer. Perhaps the
model par excellence of this operation that consists of
rendering inoperative all human works is poetry itself.
What is poetry if not an operation in language that
deactivates and renders inoperative its communicative
and informative functions in order to open them to
a new possible use? Or, in Spinoza's terms, the point
at which language, having deactivated its utilitarian
functions, rests in itself and contemplates its
potentiality to say. In this sense, Dante's *Commedia*,
Leopardi's *Canti*, and Caproni's *Il seme del piangere*
are the contemplation of the Italian language; Arnaut
Daniel's sestet is the contemplation of the Occitan
language; *Trilce* and Vallejo's posthumous poems are
the contemplation of the Spanish language; Rimbaud's
Illuminations are the contemplation of the French
language; Hölderlin's hymns and Trakl's poetry are
the contemplation of the German language.

What poetry accomplishes for the potentiality to
say, politics and philosophy must accomplish for the
potentiality to act. Rendering inoperative economic
and social operations, they show what the human
body is capable of; they open it to a new possible use.

Spinoza defined the essence of each thing as desire, the *conatus* to persevere in one's being. If I might express a minor reservation with regard to a great thinker, I would say that it now seems to me that we need to insinuate a small resistance even in this Spinozian idea—as we have seen with the act of creation. Certainly, each thing desires to persevere in its being; but, at the same time, it resists this desire; it renders it inoperative at least for an instant and contemplates. Once again, this is a resistance internal to desire, an inoperativity internal to the operation. But it alone confers on *conatus* its justice and its truth. In one word—and this is, at least in art, the decisive element—its grace.

Vortexes

The archetypal movement of water is the spiral. When the water flowing in a river encounters an obstacle, be it the branch of a tree or the pillar of a bridge, a spiral movement is generated at that point, which, if it is stabilized, assumes the form and the consistency of a vortex. The same can happen if two currents of water having different temperature or speed meet: even in this case we will see the formation of whirlpools, which seem to remain immobile in the flow of waves or currents. But the coil that is formed at the crest of a wave is itself a vortex, which, because of the force of gravity, breaks into foam.

The vortex has its rhythm, which has been compared to the movement of planets around the sun. Its interior moves at a higher speed than its external margin, just like planets rotate more or less rapidly according to their distance from the sun. In coiling, the vortex extends downward and then moves upward in a sort of intimate pulsation. Moreover, if we drop an object in the whirlpool—for example, a small piece of wood shaped like a needle—it will point in the same direction in its constant rotation, indicating a point that is, so to speak, the north of the vortex. The center around and toward which the vortex ceaselessly whirls is, however, a black sun, in which an infinite force of suction is in action. According to scientists, this can be expressed by saying that at the point of the vortex where the radius is equal to zero, pressure is equal to "minus infinity."

Let us think over the special status of singularity that defines the vortex: it is a shape that is separated from the flow of water of which it was and somehow still is part; an autonomous region closed onto itself that follows its own laws. It is strictly connected, however, with the whole in which it is immersed, made of the same matter that is continuously exchanged with the liquid mass that surrounds it. It is an independent being, yet there is no drop that separately belongs to it, and its identity is absolutely immaterial.

It is well known that Benjamin compared the origin to a vortex:

> The origin [*Ursprung*] stands in the flux of becoming as a vortex and rips into its rhythm the material of emergence [*Entstehung*]. . . . On the one hand, that which is original

wants to be recognized as restoration and reestablish-
ment, but, on the other hand, and precisely because of
this, as something incomplete and unconcluded. There
takes place in every original phenomenon a determination of the figure in which an idea will constantly
confront the historical world, until it is revealed fulfilled,
in the totality of its history. Origin is not, therefore,
discovered by the examination of actual findings, but it
is related to their pre- and post-history. . . . The category
of origin is not therefore, as Cohen holds, a purely logical
one, but a historical one.

Let us try to take seriously the image of the origin
as a vortex. First of all, the origin is no longer something that precedes becoming and remains separate
from it in chronology. Like the whirlpool in the river's
flow, the origin is simultaneous with the becoming of
phenomena, from which it derives its matter but in
which it dwells in a somehow autonomous and station-
ary way. Insofar as the origin accompanies historical
becoming, trying to understand the latter will not
mean taking it back to an origin separated in time, but
comparing and maintaining it with something that,
like a vortex, is still present in it.

We better comprehend a phenomenon if we do not
confine its origin to a remote point in time. The *arché*,
the whirling origin that archaeological investigation
tries to reach, is a historical a priori that remains

immanent to becoming and continues to act in it.
Even in the course of our life, the vortex of the origin
remains present until the end and silently accompanies
our existence at every moment. At times it gets closer;
at other times it distances itself so much that we are
no longer able to glimpse it or to perceive its hushed
swarming. But, at decisive moments, it seizes us and
drags us inside it; we then suddenly realize that we
are ourselves nothing other than a fragment of the
beginning that continues to spin in the whirlpool from
which our life derives, to swirl in it until it reaches the
point of infinite negative pressure and disappears—
unless chance spits it out again.

Beautiful

There are beings that desire only to be sucked into
the vortex of the origin. Others rather maintain with
it a reticent and cautious relation, endeavoring as far
as possible not to be swallowed up by the maelstrom.
Finally, others again, more fearful or unaware, have
not even ever dared to cast a glance at it.

The two extreme stages of liquids—and of being—
are the drop and the vortex. The drop is the point at
which the liquid separates from itself, becomes ecstatic
(by falling or splashing, water is separated into drops
at its extremities). The vortex is the point at which the

this reads like poetry

liquid concentrates itself, rotates, and sinks into itself.
There are drop-beings and vortex-beings—creatures
that with all their strength try to separate themselves
on the outside and creatures that obstinately coil
around themselves, venturing more and more into
the inside. But it is curious that even the drop, falling
back into the water, produces yet another vortex,
becoming a whirlpool and a spiral.

We should not conceive of the subject as a substance
but as a vortex in the flow of becoming. He has no
other substance than that of the single being, but,
with respect to it, he has his own figure, manner,
and movement. And it is in this sense that we need
to understand the relation between substance and its
modes. Modes are the whirlpools in the endless field of
substance, which, by collapsing and swirling in itself,
is subjectivized, becomes aware of itself, suffers and
enjoys.

Names—and each name is a proper or a divine
name—are the vortexes of the historical becoming
of languages, whirlpools in which the semantic and
communicative tension of language clogs up into itself
and becomes equal to zero. In a name, we no longer
say—or do not yet say—anything; we only call.

It is perhaps for this reason that, in the naive representation of the origin of language, we imagine that names come first, discrete and isolated as in a dictionary, and that we then combine them to form a discourse. Once again, this puerile imagination becomes perspicuous if we understand that the name is actually a vortex that perforates and interrupts the semantic flow of language, not simply in order to abolish it. In the vortex of nomination, the linguistic sign, by turning and sinking into itself, is intensified and exacerbated in the extreme; it then makes itself be sucked in at the point of infinite pressure, in which it disappears as a sign and re-emerges on the other side as a pure name. A poet is the one who plunges into this vortex, where everything becomes again for him a name. One by one he has to take back signifying words from the flow of discourse and throw them into the whirlpool, to find them again in the illustrious vernacular of the poem as names. The latter are something we reach—if we reach them—only at the end of the descent into the vortex of the origin.

In the Name of What?

Many years ago, in a country not far from Europe, in which the political situation was hopeless and the people depressed and unhappy, a few months before the revolution that led to the fall of the king, there were tapes in which one could hear a voice crying out:

> In the name of God the merciful and the compassionate! Wake up! For ten years the king has spoken of development, and yet in our nation there is a shortage of basic necessities. He makes us promises for the future, but people know that the king's promises are empty words. Both the spiritual and material conditions of the country are desperate. I call on you students, factory workers, peasants, merchants, and craftsmen, to encourage you to fight, to form an opposition movement. The end of the regime is near. Wake up! In the name of God the merciful and the compassionate!

The oppressed and unhappy people heard this voice, and the corrupted king had to flee. Even in our coun-

try people are sad and unhappy; even here political life
is dull and hopeless. But while that voice was speaking in the name of something—in the name of God
the merciful and the compassionate—in the name of
who or what can a voice here speak out? It is in fact
not enough for the one who speaks to say things that
are true and express shared opinions. For his speech to
be really heard, it has to speak in the name of something. In every discussion, in every discourse, in every
conversation, in the final analysis the decisive question
is, In the name of what are you speaking?

For centuries, even in our culture, the decisive words
have been uttered, for better or worse, in the name
of God. In the Bible, not only Moses but all the
prophets, and Jesus himself, speak in the name of
God. In this name gothic cathedrals were built, and
the frescos of the Sistine Chapel were painted; for the
love of this name Dante wrote the *Divine Comedy* and
Spinoza the *Ethics*. And even in everyday moments of
desperation or happiness, of anger or hope, it is in the
name of God that one spoke or listened to the word.
But it is also true that, in the name of God, crusades
were fought and innocents were persecuted.

Here men have long ago ceased speaking in the name of God. Prophets—perhaps for good reason—do not have a good press, and those who think and write would not like their words to be taken for prophecies. Even priests hesitate to invoke the name of God outside of liturgy. In their place, experts do speak in the name of knowledge and the technologies they represent. But to speak in the name of one's knowledge or competence is not to speak in the name of something. By definition, those who speak in the name of a knowledge or technology cannot speak beyond the limits of that knowledge or technology. Confronted with the urgency of our questions and the complexity of our situation, we obscurely feel that no partial technology or knowledge can claim to give us an answer. For this, when we are obliged to listen to the specialists and experts, we do not believe and cannot believe in their reasons. The "economy" and technology can—perhaps—replace politics, but they cannot give us the name, in the name of which to speak. For this, we can name things, but we can no longer speak *in* the name.

This is also valid for the philosopher, in case he claims to speak in the name of a knowledge that by now coincides with an academic discipline. If the word of philosophy had a sense, this was only

because it did not speak starting from knowledge but
from the awareness of non-knowledge, that is, from
the suspension of every technology and knowledge.
Philosophy is not a disciplinary field but an intensity
that can suddenly vivify any field of knowledge and
life, obliging it to come up against its own limits.
Philosophy is the state of exception declared in every
knowledge and discipline. This state of exception
is called truth. But truth is not that in the name of
which we speak; it is the content of our words. We
cannot speak in the name of truth; we can only say
what is true. In the name of what, then, can the
philosopher speak today?

This question is also valid for the poet. In the name
of whom or what, and to whom or what, can he
today speak? It has been said that the possibility of
shaking the historical existence of a people seems to
have vanished. Art, philosophy, poetry, and religion
are no longer able, at least in the West, to assume the
historical vocation of a people and encourage it to
carry out a new task—and this is not necessarily a
bad thing. Art, philosophy, poetry, and religion have
been transformed into cultural shows and have lost all
historical effectiveness. They are names of which we
speak but not words uttered in the name.

Whatever the reasons that have brought us to this, we know that, today, we can no longer talk in the name of God. And, as seen, neither can we talk in the name of truth, because truth is not a name but a discourse. It is this lack of a name that makes it so difficult for those who would have something to say to take the floor. Only the cunning and the stupid speak, and they do it in the name of the market, the crisis, pseudo-sciences, acronyms, institutions, parties, ministries, often without having anything to say.

Those who, in the end, are brave enough to speak know that they speak—or, if need be, keep silent—in the name of a name that is missing.

To speak—or to keep silent—in the name of something that is missing means to experience and make a demand [*esigenza*]. In its pure form, a demand is always a demand for a missing name. And, vice versa, the missing name demands us to speak in its name.

We say that something demands something else if the first thing is and the second will also be, but the former does not logically imply the latter or force it to exist. What a demand demands is, in fact, not the reality but the possibility of something. The possibility that becomes the object of a demand is, however, stronger than any reality. For this, the missing name demands the possibility of the word even if nobody comes forward to utter it. But the one who finally decides to speak—or to keep silent—in the name of this demand does not need, for his word or silence, any other legitimacy.

According to cabbalists, men can speak because their language contains the name of God ("name of God" is a tautology, since in Judaism God *is* the name, the *shem ha-mephorash*). The Torah is in fact nothing other than the combination of the letters of the name of God; it is literally made out of divine names. For this, according to Scholem, "the name of God is the essential name, which constitutes the origin of all languages."

Leaving aside the cabbalists' concerns, we can say that to speak in the name of God means to speak in the name of language. This, and only this, defines the dignity of the poet and the philosopher: that they speak only in the name of language. What, then, happens when, in modernity, the name of God begins to withdraw from the language of men? What is a language from which the name of God has disappeared? Hölderlin's answer—both resolute and unexpected—is: the language of poetry, the language that no longer has a name. He writes: "The poet needs no weapons and no cunning / As long as God's absence comes to his aid."

For the poet the demand had a name: the people. Like God, for whom it is often a synonym, the people are, for the poet, always the object and, at the same time, the subject of a demand. From here follows the fundamental nexus between the poet and politics, as well as the difficulty experienced by poetry at a certain point. For if the people, precisely as the object of a demand, can only be missing, it is nonetheless the case that on the threshold of modernity this lack increased and became intolerable. Hölderlin's poetry marks the point at which the poet, who lives the lack of the people—and of God—as a catastrophe, seeks refuge in philosophy and must turn into a philosopher. He thus transforms the lack into "aid" ("as long as God's absence comes to his aid"). But this attempt can be successful only if the philosopher also turns into a poet. Poetry and philosophy can in fact communicate only in the experience of the missing people. If, moving from the Greek term for "people," *demos*, we call this experience "ademy," the latter is, then, for the poet and the philosopher—or better, for the poet-philosopher or the philosopher-poet—the name of the indissoluble nexus that links poetry with philosophy—and, at the same time, the name of the politics in which he lives (the *demo*cracy in which we live today is essentially a*demy*—it is therefore an empty word).

And if the poet and the philosopher speak in the name of language, they must now speak in the name of a language without the people (this is Canetti's and Celan's project: writing in German as a language that has no relation with the German people; saving German language from its people).

The fact that Hölderlin's two friends—Hegel and Schelling—did not want to become poets (which does not mean writing poetry, but experiencing the same catastrophe that, from a certain moment, destroyed Hölderlin's language) is significant. Modern philosophy failed in its political task because it betrayed its poetic task; it did not want to put itself at risk in poetry or know how to do it. Heidegger attempted to pay the debt philosophy had in this way incurred with Hölderlin, but was not able to be a poet; he feared the "rail accident" that he believed was about to happen in his language. For this, even for him names went missing; for this, in the end, he had to invoke an unnamed god ("only a god can save us").

We can speak—or keep silent—only starting from the awareness of our ademy. But the one who had to renounce the people—and could not do otherwise— knows that he has also lost the name of the word; he knows that he can no longer speak in its name. That is, he knows—without regret or resentment—that politics has lost its place, that the categories of the political have collapsed everywhere. *Ademy, anomie,* and *anarchy* are synonyms. But it is only by trying to name the desert that grows in the absence of the name that he will—perhaps—again find the word. If the name was the name of language, he now speaks in a language without name. Only he who has long kept silent in the name can speak in the without-name, the without-law, the without-people. Anonymously, anarchically, aprosodically. Only he has access to the coming politics and poetry.

Easter in Egypt

For reasons that I hope will become evident, I would like to entitle these brief comments "Easter in Egypt." There is, in fact, a sentence in the correspondence between Ingeborg Bachmann and Paul Celan that very much struck me. I do not know if it has already been noted, but it seems to me that it allows us to position Celan's life and poetry in a new way (the life *and* poetry that he never wanted to or could separate).

The sentence in question can be found in Celan's letter to Max Frisch dated April 15, 1959, which answers Frisch and Ingeborg Bachmann's invitation to visit them in Uetikon. In declining, or rather postponing their invitation, Celan explains that he has to go to London "to visit an old aunt . . . for Jewish Easter," and he adds: "though I by no means recall ever escaping from Egypt, I will celebrate [this festival] in England."[1]

"Though I by no means recall ever escaping from Egypt, I will celebrate [this festival] in England." I want to try and think about the Impossible, and almost the Unthinkable, that is contained in this sentence, as well as about the paradoxical situation of Judaism (and of Celan in Judaism) that is implicit in it.

Celan positions himself as a Jew in Egypt, that is to say, before or anyway outside of the exodus of the Jews from Egypt under the leadership of Moses, which the Jewish Easter commemorates and celebrates.

This is something much more radical than a claim for *galut*, for exile and diaspora, which Jews usually date back to the second destruction of the Temple. Celan locates himself outside of the exodus, in a Judaism deprived of Moses and of the Law. He has stayed in Egypt; it is unclear on what grounds, whether as a prisoner, a free man, or a slave, but certainly his only abode is Egypt. I do not think it is possible to imagine a Judaism that is more extraneous to the Zionist ideal.

It is only after reading this sentence that I have understood another statement made by Celan—which was reported to me by the great painter Avigdor

Arikha, who was himself born in Czernowitz and
deported. These were the years of the first conflicts
in Palestine, and Avigdor, who had enlisted in the
Zionist army, exhorted Celan to do the same for their
common homeland. Celan's answer was simply: "My
homeland is Bukovina." I recall that Arikha, telling
me this episode many years later, could not at all
understand the meaning of such a statement. How
could a Jew claim that his homeland was Bukovina?

I believe that, if he had known Celan's sentence
about his non-exit from Egypt, Avigdor would have
understood. For the one who stayed in Egypt, not
even Jerusalem, the Davidic city, can be called homeland. For this, when in a poem of 1968 or 1969 Celan
invokes Jerusalem ("Stand up Jerusalem and / raise
yourself"), he refers to himself as "the one who cut the
tie to you" (the German is even stronger: *wer das Band
zerschnitt zu dir hin*, "slashed the bond unto you").
Recalling Celan's brief but intense visit to Jerusalem
a few months before his death, Ilana Shmueli writes:
"He knew that he did not belong here either; he was
painfully struck by it and almost fled."

In addition to this paradoxical position in an Egyptian
Judaism, the sentence contains another and more
vertiginous impossibility: Celan, who has never left
Egypt, and who lives everywhere—in Paris, London,

Czernowitz, or Jerusalem—as if he were in Egypt, has to celebrate Pesach, the festivity that commemorates the exit from Egypt.

I would like to draw your attention to this impossible task—celebrating Pesach in Egypt—since I believe that it allows us to locate the place not only of Celan's life but also, and especially, of his poetry.

At this point it is far from surprising that the correspondence with Ingeborg opens with a poem dedicated to her whose (underlined) title is "<u>In Egypt</u>." Like all of Celan's poetry, this poem is written in Egypt and addressed to a "foreigner" who, as a subsequent letter informs us, will somehow become the foundation of and justification for writing poetry in Egypt.[2]

I believe there is an essential connection between celebrating Easter in Egypt and the situation of Celan's poetry. They communicate in the same atopia whose name is: Egypt.

This connection becomes even more evident if we recall the particular importance that the term *Pesach*, "Easter," had for Celan. You will know that every orthodox Jew receives a secret name eight days after he is born, his "Jewish name," which is transmitted only orally and used especially in religious celebrations.

Celan, who was registered in his birth certificate as Paul, received eight days later the secret name Pesach.

His name in Abraham's alliance was therefore Pesach
(not Paul) Antschel. One year before dying, Celan still
recalled it to Ilana Shmueli "with solemnity." This fact
is well known, but perhaps few know that he commit-
ted suicide, in April 1970, precisely during the Pesach
celebrations.

Celan, who never left Egypt, is thus forced by his
very name into the impossible task of celebrating
Easter in Egypt. His poetry—like his name—is this
"Easter in Egypt."

But what is an Easter—that is, a commemoration of
the exodus—that is celebrated by staying in Egypt?

I believe all that Celan has repeatedly written on the
impossibility and, at the same time, the necessity of
his poetic duty—on his dwelling in falling silent and,
at the same time, on the traversal of this falling silent
(a duty that Ingeborg, the "foreigner," seems to duly
share from beginning to end); I believe that this duty
is clarified remarkably if we relate it to the celebration
of Easter in Egypt.

"Easter in Egypt" is, in this sense, the rubric under
which the entirety of Paul (Pesach) Celan's work is
inscribed.

On the Difficulty of Reading

It is not about reading and the risks that it entails that I would like to talk but rather of an underlying risk, that is, of the difficulty or impossibility of reading; I want to try and talk not of reading but of unreadability.

All of us have experienced moments when we would like to read but cannot—in which we obstinately flip through the pages of a book, but it literally falls from our hands.

In the treatises on the life of monks, this was actually the risk par excellence to which the monk succumbed: sloth, the meridian demon, the most terrible temptation that threatens the *homines religiosi* manifests itself especially in the impossibility of reading. Here is the description provided by Saint Nilus:

When the slothful monk tries to read, he stops agitated and, soon after, drifts off to sleep; he rubs his face with his hands, stretches the fingers and reads a couple of lines, mumbling the end of each word he reads; meanwhile, he fills his head with idle calculations, counts the number of pages he still has to read and the sheets of notebooks; he hates letters and the pretty miniatures he has before his eyes, until finally he closes the book and uses it as a pillow for his head, falling into a brief and deep sleep.

Here the soul's health coincides with the readability of the book (which, in the Middle Ages, is also the book of the world), sin with the impossibility of reading, the becoming unreadable of the world.

In this sense, Simone Weil spoke of a reading of the world and of a non-reading, an opacity that resists every interpretation and hermeneutics. I would like to suggest to you to pay attention to your moments of non-reading and opacity, when the book of the world falls from your hands, since the impossibility of reading concerns you as much as reading and is perhaps equally or more instructive than it.

There is also another more radical impossibility of reading, which not so many years ago was totally common. I am referring to illiterates, these men who have been too quickly forgotten, who, at least in Italy, were the majority of the population only a century ago. A great Peruvian poet of the twentieth century has written in one of his poems: *por el analfabeto a quien escribo*, "for the illiterate to whom I write." It is important to understand the meaning of this "for": it should be understood not so much as "so that the illiterate may read me," given that by definition he will never be able to, but rather as "in his place"— like when Primo Levi used to say that he witnessed for those who were called Muslims in the Auschwitz jargon, that is, those who could not or would not have been able to witness, since, shortly after entering the camp, they had lost all consciousness and sensibility.

I would like you to think about the special status of a book that is aimed at eyes that cannot read it and was written with a hand that, in a certain sense, does not know how to write. The poet or the writer who writes for the illiterates or the Muslims tries to write what cannot be read; they put on paper the unreadable. But it is precisely this that makes their writing more interesting than that which was written for only those who can read.

There is, then, another case of non-reading I would like to talk about. I am referring to books that have not found what Benjamin called the time of their readability, books that were written and published

but are—perhaps forever—waiting to be read. I know
books that are worth reading but have not been read,
or have been read by too few readers—I think all of
you could name books of this kind. What is the status
of these books? I think that if these books are really
good, we should not be speaking of a waiting but of a
demand [*esigenza*]. These books are not waiting, but
demand to be read, even if they have not been read
and will never be read. Demand is a very interesting
concept, which does not refer to the field of facts but
to a superior and more decisive sphere, whose nature is
up to you to specify.

But then I would like to give some advice to pub-
lishers and those who deal with books: stop looking
at the infamous—yes, infamous—best-seller charts
and rather try to construct in your mind the chart of
the books that demand to be read. Only a publishing industry founded on such a mental chart could
overcome the crisis that—I hear repeated—books are
facing.

A poet once summarized his poetics with the
following formula: "To read what was never written."
As you can see, this is an experience somehow
symmetrical to that of the poet who writes for the
illiterate who cannot read him: a writing without
reading corresponds here to a reading without writing,

provided we specify that time is also reversed: a
writing that is not followed by any reading, in the first
case; a reading that is not preceded by any writing, in
the second.

But maybe what is at stake in both these formulations is something similar, that is, an experience
of writing and reading that puts into question the
representation we usually have of these strictly related
activities, which oppose and at the same time refer to
something unreadable and impossible to write that
preceded them and does not stop accompanying them.

You have probably guessed that I am referring to
orality. Our literature was born in an intimate relation
to orality. What else is Dante doing when he decides
to write in vernacular, if not writing what has never
been read and reading what has never been written,
that is, that illiterate "maternal speech," which existed
only in the oral dimension? His attempt to put down
in writing the maternal speech obliges him not only to
transcribe it but, as you know, to invent that language
of poetry, that illustrious vernacular, which does
not exist anywhere and whose scent, like that of the
panther of medieval bestiaries, "is left everywhere but
is nowhere to be seen."

I think it is not possible to understand the great
flourishing of twentieth-century Italian poetry if we

do not perceive in it something of an echo of that unreadable orality that, Dante says, "one and alone is first in the mind"—that is, if we do not understand that it is accompanied by the equally extraordinary flourishing of poetry in dialects. Perhaps Italian literature of the twentieth century is entirely traversed by an unwitting memory, almost by a laborious commemoration of illiteracy. Those who have held one of these books in their hands, in which the page written—or, better, transcribed—in dialect is juxtaposed to the Italian translation, cannot but ask, as their eyes skim restlessly through the pages, whether the real place of poetry is in neither one nor the other page but in the empty space between them.

I would like to close these brief remarks on the difficulty of reading by asking you whether what we call poetry is not actually something that incessantly inhabits, works, and underlies written language so as to give it back to that unreadable from which it comes and toward which it travels.

From the Book to the Screen: The Before and the After of the Book

Roland Barthes's last course at the Collège de France is entitled *The Preparation of the Novel.* Right at the beginning, as if it were an omen of his imminent death, Barthes evokes the moment in life when we start to realize that being mortal is no longer a vague feeling but a fact. At the same time, he recalls his decision, taken a few months earlier, to devote himself to a new way of writing, to "write as if I'd never written before."

The theme of the course somehow corresponds to this decision. Barthes summarizes it with the formula "wanting-to-write," which designates the "poorly defined, and poorly studied" period that precedes the drafting of a work. In particular, given that the course is dedicated to the "preparation of the novel," he evokes, without scrutinizing it, the problem of the relation between "the fantasy of the novel" and the preparatory notes, the fragments, and, at last, the passage from the fragmented novel to the novel proper.

This very important and "poorly studied" theme is, however, soon abandoned, and Barthes unexpectedly moves on to treat Japanese haiku, a poetic genre we know only in its rigidly codified form—the least appropriate topic one can imagine given the investigation announced by the title of the course (which could rather be condensed in the formula "the before of the book or the text").

I will use this formula—"the before of the book"—to refer to all that precedes the finished book and work, to that limbo, that pre- or sub-world of fantasies, sketches, notes, copybooks, drafts, blotters to which our culture is not able to give a legitimate status nor an adequate graphic design—probably because our idea of creation and work is encumbered with the theological paradigm of the divine creation of the world, that incomparable *fiat*, which, according to the theologians, is not a *facere de materia* but a *creare ex nihilo*, a creation that is not only not preceded by any matter but is instantaneously accomplished, without hesitation or second thoughts, through a gratuitous and immediate act of the will. Before creating the world, God did not prepare any draft or take notes; rather, the problem of the "before of the creation," the question about what God was doing before creating the world is, in theology, a forbidden topic. The Christian God is to such an extent an essentially and constitutively creative God, that to pagans and Gnostics who asked him this embarrassing question Augustine could only ironically reply with a threat, which actually betrays an impossibility of answering: "God cut rods to beat those who ask impertinent questions."

Whatever the view of Augustine—and of Luther, who many centuries later returned to the topic using almost identical words—even in theology things are not really that simple. According to a tradition of Platonic origin, which exerted a profound influence on the Renaissance conception of artistic creation, God always had in his mind the ideas of all the creatures he then created. Even though we cannot speak of a matter or of an outline, there is in God something that precedes creation, an immemorial "before" the work, which would have been frantically accomplished in the biblical Hexameron. In Cabala, too, there is a tradition according to which the fact that God created the world out of nothing means that nothingness is the matter with which he made his creation, that is, that the divine work is literally made of nothing.

It is over this obscure pre-world, this impure and
prohibited matter, that I would like to cast a glance, first
of all in order to put into question the way in which we
usually think not only the act of creation but also the
finished work and the book in which it takes shape.

In 1927 Francesco Moroncini published his critical edition of Leopardi's *Canti*. This is one of the
first times that, instead of limiting himself to pro-
viding the critical text of each poem, a philologist
has reproduced—thanks to a series of typographical
devices—not only the manuscript of each canto in its
materiality and in all of its particulars, with the cor-
rections, variants, notes, and comments of the author,
but also the early versions and, where it exists, the
initial prose version [*"getto in prosa"*]. The reader is initially disoriented because the perfect compositions he
was used to reading in one shot now lose their familiar
consistency; they expand and extend page after page,
allowing him in this way to retrace the temporal process that led to their drafting. But, at the same time,
when prolonged in time and space, the poem seems to
have lost its identity and place: where are *Le ricor-
danze*, *Canto notturno*, and *L'infinito*? Brought back to
the process of their genesis, they are no longer readable as a unitary whole, just as we could not recognize
a portrait in which a painter expected to represent
together the different ages of the same face.

I have mentioned the initial prose versions, which, in some cases—for instance, *L'inno ai patriarchi*—have been preserved. What are these enigmatic pages in prose, which seem an awkward and badly written paraphrase of the *Canti* yet contain, in all likelihood, the magmatic and burning kernel, almost the living embryo, of poetry? How should we read them? With an eye on the finished text so as to try and understand in which way a perfect organism developed out of such an insignificant fragment—or as such, as if they miraculously contracted in a few lines the springing sprout and the dictation of poetry?

Things get even more complex if we think of those sketches and outlines, both in literature and the visual arts, where the original sprout was not followed by a finished work. Kafka's diaries are full of—at times extremely short—beginnings of tales that were never written, and in the history of art we often encounter sketches that we have to suppose refer to paintings that were never painted. Do we need here to evoke the absent work, arbitrarily projecting the sketches and the notes into an imaginary future, or rather, as seems fairer, appreciate them as such? It is evident that this question implies that the difference, which we take for granted, between the completed work and the fragment is revoked without reservation. For example, what distinguishes Simone Weil's books and published articles from her notebooks and posthumous fragments, which many consider her most important work—or, anyway, that in which she expressed herself most exhaustively? In his little masterpiece *Art and Anarchy*, Edgar Wind recalls that the Romantics, from Friedrich Schlegel to Novalis, were convinced that fragments and outlines were superior to the completed work and, for this reason, intentionally left their writings in a fragmentary form. Michelangelo's intention was not very different when he decided to leave unfinished the sculptures of the Sagrestia Nova.

In this perspective, it is instructive to note that over the last decades we have witnessed a radical change in ecdotics, the science that deals with the edition of texts. In the tradition of Lachmannian philology, editors aimed in the past at reconstructing a single and, as far as possible, definitive critical text. If you take a look at the great edition of Hölderlin's works recently finalized in Germany, or at that of Kafka's works, which is still in progress, you know that, pushing to the limit Moroncini's method, they reproduce all the layers of the manuscript without distinguishing between the different versions and without relegating any longer the rejected variants and forms to the critical notes. This entails a decisive transformation in the way in which we conceive the identity of a work. None of the various versions is the "text" because the latter presents itself as a potentially infinite temporal process—both toward the past, of which it includes every outline, draft, and fragment, and toward the future—whose interruption at a certain point in its history, for biographical reasons or the author's decision, is purely contingent. In his book *A Giacometti Portrait*,[1] James Lord often recalls that Giacometti never tired of repeating, as Cézanne had already done, that one never finishes a painting, but simply abandons it.

The caesura, which puts an end to the drafting of a work, does not confer on it a privileged status of completeness: it only means that the work can be said to be finished when, through interruption or abandonment, it is constituted as a fragment of a potentially infinite creative process, with respect to which the so-called completed work is distinguished only accidentally from the uncompleted one.

If this is the case, if each work is essentially a fragment, it will be legitimate to speak not only of a "before" but also of an "after" of the book, which is equally problematic and even less studied.

In 427, three years before dying, and after having already produced a vast work, Augustine writes *Retractationes*. The term *retraction*—even when it is not used in the juridical sense of taking back a statement given at a trial or declaring it untrue—has today only the pejorative meaning of recanting or repudiating what one has said or written. Augustine rather uses it in the sense of "treating anew." He humbly returns to the books he has written not only, or not primarily, to amend their flaws and imprecisions but to clarify their meanings and aims; for this, he takes up again and somehow continues their writing.

Almost fifteen centuries later, between the end of 1888 and the beginning of 1889, Nietzsche repeats Augustine's gesture and returns to the books he has written but with an emotionally opposed approach. The title he uses for his "retraction," *Ecce Homo*, is certainly antiphrastic, since the words with which Pontius Pilate presents Jesus to the Jews—a naked and flagellated Jesus who is wearing a crown of thorns— are here turned into a self-glorification without limits or reservations. After declaring that in a certain sense he considers himself to be already dead, like his father, he asks "why I write such good books" and, retracing one after the other the books he has written up to that point, not only explains how and why they originated but also suggests, with the authority of the *auctor*, how they need to be read and what he really meant to say.

In both cases, *retraction* supposes that the author can continue to write the books he has already written, as if they remained until the end fragments of a work in progress, which for this reason tends to blend with life. A similar intention must have motivated the legendary gesture of Bonnard: we are told that, armed with a brush, he used to visit the museums in which his paintings were exhibited, and, taking advantage of the attendants' absence, he adjusted and improved them. The theological paradigm of divine creation shows here its other face, according to which creation was not accomplished on the sixth day but continues infinitely, since if God ceased to create the world even only for one moment, it would be destroyed.

Among the Italian writers and filmmakers of the twentieth century, there is one who has practiced retraction in all senses of the term—even the technical-juridical one, given that at one point in his life he rejected and "abjured" a considerable part of his work: Pier Paolo Pasolini. In his case, however, retraction becomes so complex that it assumes a paradoxical form. In 1992 Einaudi published a lengthy posthumous work by Pasolini, entitled *Petrolio*. The book—if one can speak of a book—is made up of 133 numbered fragments, followed by critical annotations and a letter to Alberto Moravia. The letter is important because Pasolini explains in it how he conceived the "novel" in question; he soon adds that

it "is not written like real novels are written" but as
an essay, a review, a private letter, or a critical edition.
This last definition is the crucial one. In a 1973 note,
which the editors have inserted at the beginning of
the book, he in fact specifies that "*Petrolio* as a whole
(from the second draft) should be presented as a
critical edition of an unpublished text, of which only
fragments are preserved, in four or five discordant
manuscripts." The coincidence between completed
and unfinished work here is absolute: the author
writes a book in the guise of a critical edition of an
uncompleted book. Not only does the uncompleted
text become indiscernible from the completed one, but
also, with a peculiar contraction of times, the author
identifies with the philologist who should provide its
posthumous edition.

In the letter to Moravia, there is a passage of particular significance in which the author-editor states that
this is not a novel but the re-evocation [*rievocazione*] of
an unwritten novel:

> Everything that is novelistic in this novel is so as a re-
> evocation of the novel. If I gave substance to what is here
> only potential, if, that is, I invented the writing necessary
> to make this story an object, a narrative machine that
> functions by itself in the reader's imagination, I would
> necessarily have to accept that conventionality which is,
> ultimately, a game. I have no further desire to play.

Whatever the biographical reasons that led to Paso-lini's choice, we are at any rate facing an uncompleted book that is presented as the "re-evocation" or the retraction of a work that was never thought as a work, that is, as something that the author intended to complete. *Re-evocation* equally means here "revoca-tion": the absent novel is re-evoked (or, rather, evoked) through its revocation as novel. Yet it is only in rela-tion to this unwritten work that the published frag-ments acquire their meaning—even if just ironically.

Facing cases like this, it is possible to assess the insufficiency of the categories through which our culture has accustomed us to think the ontological status of the book and the work. Starting at least with Aristotle, we think the work (which the Greeks called *ergon*) by relating two concepts: potentiality and actuality, virtual and real (in Greek, *dynamis* and *energeia*, being-at-work). The current idea, accepted as obvious, is that the possible and the virtual—the "before" of the work—precede the actual and the real, the *ergon*, the completed work, in which what was only possible finds its realization through an act of the will. This means that, in outlines and notes, potentiality has not been transferred to the act and has not been integrally exhausted in it; the "wanting-to-write" has remained unrealized and uncompleted.

me as + ru

In *Petrolio*, however, according to all evidence, the possible or virtual book does not precede its real fragments but claims to coincide with them—and these are nothing other than the re-evocation or revocation of the possible book. Is it not the case that every book contains a remainder of potentiality, without which its reading and reception would be impossible? A work in which creative potentiality were totally extinguished would not be a work but the ashes and sepulcher of the work. If we really want to comprehend that curious object that is a book, we need to complicate the relation between potentiality and actuality, possible and real, matter and form, and try to imagine a possible that takes place only in the real and a real that does not stop becoming possible. It is perhaps only this hybrid creature, this non-place in which potentiality does not disappear but is preserved and, so to speak, dances in the act, that deserves the name of "work." If the author can go back to his work, if the before and the after of the work do not simply need to be forgotten, this is not because, like the Romantics believed, the fragment and the sketch are more important than the work; rather, it is because the experience of matter—which for the ancients was a synonym for potentiality—is immediately perceivable in them.

In this perspective, there are two exemplary literary works that propose themselves as "books" in an eminent way, but in which this atopia and almost ontological inconsistency of the book are nonetheless pushed to their extreme limit. The first is Giorgio Manganelli's *Nuovo commento*, published in 1969 by Einaudi and republished in 1993 by Adelphi. The publishing house Adelphi has certainly many merits, yet in the case of Manganelli it has demonstrated itself to be unscrupulous, by removing the author's blurbs from the books it was republishing—which, like any reader of Manganelli knows, are an integral part of it—and then collecting them as a separate volume. This time, however, for the republication of *Nuovo commento*, Adelphi has felt the need to reproduce in a special appendix both the blurb and the cover illustration of the original edition, to which the blurb refers, and which represents, in the words of the author, an immobile alphabetical explosion of letters, ideograms, and typographical symbols, of which the book would be the support or commentary. In fact, *Nuovo commento* presents itself as a series of notes about an inexistent text—or, rather, of notes about notes without a text, which are at times extremely lengthy notes to a punctuation mark (such as a semicolon), and which, occupying an entire page, become—one does not really know how—actual tales. Manganelli's hypothesis is not only that of the inexistence of the text but—also and in equal measure—that of the, so to speak, theological autonomy of the commentary. Precisely for this, one cannot simply say that the text is missing: rather, it is in a certain sense—like God—everywhere and nowhere; it includes its own commentary or makes itself be included by it, so as to become imperceptible, like an interlinear gloss that cancels or devours the lines of the sacred text on which it comments.

Perhaps the best definition of Manganelli's book is contained in a passage from a letter that Italo Calvino wrote to the author, describing his impressions as a reader:

> One starts by saying: I've already understood everything; this is a commentary on a text that does not exist; too bad the game is clear from the beginning; I wonder how he will be able to continue this for so many pages without any narration. . . . Then, when we no longer expect it, we receive the golden gift of actual narrations; at a certain point, through a process of accumulation, we pass a certain threshold and reach a sudden revelation: of course, the *text* is God and the universe, how could I not have realized it any earlier? Then one reads it again with the key that the *text* is the universe as language, the discourse of a God that does not refer to any signi- fied but to the sum of signifiers, and everything makes perfect sense.[2]

In this theological reading, the *Nuovo commento* is identified with the universe (the book-world is, after all, a well-known Medieval *topos*) and with God—but with a God that rather resembles that of the cabbalistic tradition, who originally created the Torah not as names and meaningful propositions but as an incoherent mixture of letters without order or articulation. Only after Adam's sin, God arranged the letters of the unreadable original Torah (the Torah of *Atzilut*) to form the words of the Book of books (the Torah of *Beriʾah*); but, precisely for this reason, the coming of the Messiah will coincide with the restoration of the Torah, in which words will explode and letters will be given back to their pure materiality, to their meaningless (or omnisignificant) disorder.

In Manganelli's book, there follows the decisive importance of the illustration on the cover, which, curiously, Calvino did not notice. At the very moment at which it identifies with the world and with God, the book explodes—or implodes—into a dissemination of letters and typographical signs. As the explosion of a book, however, it has a square-shaped form; that is, it maintains the shape of a page—but of a purely unreadable page, which, being identical with the world, no longer presupposes any reference to it.

There also follows the proximity between *Nuovo commento* and the book that ostensibly stands as its archetype: Mallarmé's so-called *livre*. In 1957, almost sixty years after the death of the poet, Jacques Scherer publishes with Gallimard a book whose title in the frontispiece reads: *Le "Livre" de Mallarmé*. Above the title, which attributes the book in question to Mallarmé, the name of the author is Jacques Scherer. The position of the author is actually undecidable because the unreadable unpublished manuscript, formed of 202 handwritten notes taken by Mallarmé, is preceded by a text of equal length by the editor—a sort of metaphysical isagoge not indexed as such—and followed by another text, in which Scherer proposes a "staging" of the "book," made up of the words and the sentences contained in the notes, but ordered by the editor so as to form a sort of play or theatrical mystery.

It is known that Mallarmé, convinced that "the world exists only to end up in a book," pursued throughout his life the project of an absolute book, in which chance—*le hasard*—had to be eliminated point by point from all levels of the literary process. For this, it was first of all necessary to eliminate the author, since "the pure work implies the elocutionary disappearance of the poet." It was then necessary to abolish chance in words, since each of them results from the contingent union of a sound and a meaning.

How? By including the casual elements in a necessary and vaster set: initially, the verse "that out of several terms re-forges a total word, new, alien to natural language"; then, in an increasing *crescendo*, the page, constituted—following the impure example of the advertising *affiche*, to which Mallarmé paid a lot of attention—as a new poetic unity in a simultaneous vision, including blank spaces and the words disseminated on it; and finally, the "book," no longer understood as a material readable object but as a play, a theatrical mystery, or a virtual operation that coincides with the world. It seems that Mallarmé was thinking of a kind of performance or dance, in which twenty-four readers-spectators would have read twenty-four sheets of paper always arranged in a different order. Judging from the book published by Scherer, the result is that the book-world explodes at this point into a series of unreadable sheets, full of signs, words, digits, calculations, points, and graphemes. The manuscript nestled in the *livre* is, in fact, partly a mishmash of arduous calculations, consisting of multiplications, sums, and equations, and partly a series of "instructions for use," both meticulous and inapplicable.

The "throw of the dice" of the "book" that has claimed to identify with the world eliminates chance only on the condition of making the book-world explode into a palingenesis that is itself necessarily casual. As with the end of the world of the Christian tradition, the last day is the integral recapitulation of what is destroyed and lost forever: the *ekpyrosis*, the consummation by fire, coincides with the *anakephalaiosis*, the punctual recapitulation of everything.

At this point, it should be clear that the book is—or at least claims to be—something far less solid and reassuring than we are used to. In Manganelli's words, "its presence has become so elusive and aggressive that it can be nowhere and everywhere"; as was Mallarmé's intention, it has been completely realized by becoming absolutely virtual. The "book" is what does not take place either in the book or in the world, and, for this, it must destroy the world and itself.

After this brief metaphysical digression, we should try to investigate the material history and, so to speak, the "physics" of the book—which is in turn more difficult than it seems at first sight. The book as we know it appears in Europe between the fourth and fifth century of the Christian era. This is the moment when the *codex*—the technical term for "book" in Latin—replaces the *volumen* and the scroll, which were the normal form of the book in Antiquity. It is enough to think for a moment to realize that this was an actual revolution. The *volumen* was a scroll of papyrus (and later of parchment), which the reader unrolled with the right hand, holding in the left the part that contained the *umbilicus*, that is, the wooden or ebony cylinder around which the volume was coiled. In the Middle Ages the *rotulus* was added, which was rather unrolled vertically from top to bottom, and was reserved for theater and ceremonies.

What happens in the passage from the *volumen* to the *codex*, whose archetype was the wax tablets used by the ancients to note down thoughts, make calculations, and for other private purposes? The codex introduces something absolutely new, to which we are so accustomed that we forget the decisive importance it had in the material and spiritual culture, and even the imagination, of the West: the page. The unrolling of the volume revealed a homogeneous and continuous space, filled with a series of juxtaposed written columns. The codex—or what we call today the book—replaces this continuous space with a discontinuous series of clearly delimited unities—the pages on which the dark or crimson column of writing is framed on each side by a blank margin. The perfectly continuous *volumen* embraced the entire text like the sky embraces the constellations that are inscribed in it; the page as a discontinuous and self-sufficient unity separates at each turn an element of the text from the others, which our gaze perceives as an isolated whole, and

the page

which needs to physically disappear in order to allow us to read the following page.

There were certainly practical reasons that contributed to the supremacy of the book, which progressively replaced the volume: it was handier; there was the possibility of isolating and finding passages of a text much more easily and, thanks to the multiplication of pages, a greater capacity for content. For instance, it is obvious that, without the page, Mallarmé's project of *livre* could not have been conceived. But there were also more essential reasons, even theological ones. Historians have noted that the diffusion of the codex happens especially in Christian milieus and goes together with that of Christianity. The most ancient manuscripts of the New Testament, which date back to a time when the primacy of the codex was not yet a foregone conclusion, are shaped like codices, not volumes. In this sense, it has been observed that the book corresponded to the linear conception of time specific of the Christian world, while the volume, with its rolling, conformed better to the cyclical conception of time typical of Antiquity. The time of reading somehow reproduced the experience of the time of life and of the cosmos; flipping through the pages of a book was not the same thing as unrolling a *volumen.*

There could also be another, strictly theological, reason for the decline and progressive disappearance of the volume in the Christian world, which somehow reflects the conflict and break between the church and the synagogue. In synagogues, on the wall directed toward Jerusalem, Jews keep the Ark of the Law, *aron ha-qodesh,* which contains the text of the Torah. This text always has the shape of a *volumen.* For Jews the sacred text is a roll; for Christians it is a book. Obviously, Jews, too, use printed editions of the Torah in the form of a book: but the transcendent archetype of these books is a *volumen,* not a *codex.* In contrast, the New Testament, as well as the Roman Missal and any other liturgical text of Christians, is in its shape not different from a profane book.

In any case, independently of the reasons that have led to the triumph of the book, the page acquires in the Christian West a symbolic meaning that promotes it to the rank of an actual *imago mundi* and *imago vitae.* When opened, the book of life or of the world always reveals the page, written or painted in miniature: in opposition to it the blank page becomes the symbol, both distressing and productive, of pure possibility. In his treatise on the soul, Aristotle compared the potentiality of thought to a writing tablet on which nothing has yet been written and everything can be written: in modern culture, the blank page symbolizes the pure virtuality of writing, before which the despaired poet or novelist invokes the inspiration that will allow him to translate it into reality.

What happens today, when the book and the page seem to have given way to IT tools? Apparently, differences and similarities, analogies and anomalies, seem to overlap. Like the book, the computer enables pagination, but, at least until its most recent developments, which allow us to "browse" the text, this did not take place like in a book but like in a roll, from top to bottom. From the theological perspective we have just recalled, the computer appears somewhere between the Roman Missal and the roll of the *aron ha-qodesh*, a sort of Judeo-Christian hybrid—and this could only have contributed to its almost indisputable primacy.

There are, however, some deeper differences and analogies, which we need to clarify. According to a careless commonplace we often hear, what is at stake in the passage from the book to digital tools is a passage from the material to the virtual. The tacit presupposition is that the material and the virtual designate two opposite dimensions and that the virtual is synonymous with the immaterial. Both these presuppositions are, if not completely false, at least very imprecise.

The Italian word *libro* [book] derives from a Latin term that originally means "wood, bark." In Greek the term for "matter" is *hyle*, which itself means "wood, forest"—or, as the Latins translate it: *silva* or *materia*, which is the term used for wood as a construction material, as different from *lignum*, that is, firewood. But for the classical world matter is the very place of possibility and virtuality: it is even pure possibility, the "shapelessness" that can receive and contain all forms, and of which form is somehow the trace. In other words, following the image given by Aristotle we have mentioned, matter is the blank page, the writing tablet on which everything can be written.

What happens to this blank page, this pure matter, in the computer? In a certain sense the computer is nothing other than a blank page, which has been fixed on that object we call, using a term on which it is worth reflecting, "screen." This word, which derives from the Ancient German verb *skirmjan*, meaning "to protect, to shelter, to defend," makes an early appearance in Italian, and in an eminent place. In the fifth chapter of the *Vita Nuova*, Dante tells us he has decided to hide his love for Beatrice, creating a "schermo de la veritade," a screen of the truth, through another lady. The metaphor is certainly optical, since the lady in question happened to be by chance on "the straight line which, parting from the most gentle Beatrice, ended in my eyes," so that the people present believed Dante's gaze was directed at her, not at Beatrice. Dante uses the term *screen* several times in the sense of protection and of a material obstacle, as when he says that, in order to protect their lands, the Flemish "make screens to oppose the sea," or when he describes the soul, which, like an angelical butterfly, "flies without screens towards Justice."

How could a word that means "obstacle, shelter" acquire the meaning of "surface on which images appear"? What is that which we call screen? What is it in digital tools that so tenaciously captures our gaze? The important thing about them is that the page as material support of writing has been separated from the page as text. In a book that everybody should read, *In the Vineyard of the Text*, Ivan Illich has shown how, already starting in the twelfth century, a series of minor technical improvements allowed monks to imagine the text as something autonomous from the physical reality of the page. But the page, which etymologically derives from a term that designated the vine shoot, was still for them a material reality, in which the gaze could "stroll" and move around to gather the characters of writing like the hand gathers a bunch of grapes (*legere*, to read, originally meant "to gather").

In digital tools the text, that is, the page as writing—codified through a numerical code that is unreadable to the human eye—has been completely emancipated from the page as support and is limited to transiting like a ghost on the screen. This break in the relation between the page and writing, which defined the book, generated the—to say the least inaccurate—idea of an immateriality of the space of information technology. What rather happens is that the screen, the material "obstacle," remains invisible and unseen in what it makes us see. That is, the computer is constructed in such a way that readers never see the screen as such, in its materiality, because as soon as we switch it on, it fills up with characters, symbols, or images. When we use a computer, an iPad, or Kindle, we keep our eyes fixed for hours on a screen that we never see as such. If we perceive the screen, that is, if the screen is blank, or, worse, if it turns black, this means that the tool is not functioning. As in the Platonic doctrine of matter, which the ancients deemed particularly difficult to understand, matter, the *chora*, is here what gives way to all sensible forms without being perceived.

Digital devices are not immaterial but founded on the obliteration of their own materiality: the screen "screens" itself, hides the page as support—that is, matter—in the page as writing, which has itself become immaterial or, rather, spectral—if by specter we mean something that has lost its body but also somehow preserves the form of its body. Those who use these devices are readers and writers who, without realizing it, had to forgo the—both distressing and productive—experience of the blank page, of that writing tablet on which nothing is yet written, which Aristotle compared with the pure potentiality of thought.

At this point, I would like to propose a minimal definition of thought, which seems to me particularly pertinent. *To think means to recall the blank page while we write or read.* To think—but also to read—means to recall matter. And just as Manganelli's and Mallarmé's books were perhaps nothing other than an attempt at bringing back the book to the pure materiality of the blank page, so those who use computers should be able to neutralize its fiction of immateriality—which originates from the fact that the screen, the material "obstacle," the shapelessness of which all shapes are the trace, remains to them obstinately invisible.

Opus Alchymicum

Claudio Rugafiori has entitled his edition of a collection of letters by René Daumal *Il lavoro su di sé* [*The Work on Oneself*]. His thesis is clear and enunciated without reservations: the author in question did not really intend to produce literary works but rather to act on himself, so as to transform and recreate himself (Daumal also speaks of "coming out of sleep, awakening"). That is, writing is part of an ascetic practice in which the *production of work* becomes secondary with respect to the *transformation of the subject* who writes. As Daumal confides to his teacher Jeanne de Salzmann, "Naturally, this renders my work as a writer much more arduous, but also far more interesting and spiritually fruitful. . . . Work becomes always more a 'work *on* myself,' rather than a work '*for* myself.'"[1]

From the outset, when he animated with Roger Gilbert-Lecomte the journal *Le Grand Jeu*, Daumal's practice of writing was accompanied—or, rather, guided—by experiences that do not seem to have at first sight anything to do with literature (one of the most extreme was inhaling the vapors of carbon tetrachloride until losing consciousness, in an attempt to grasp the threshold between consciousness and unconsciousness, life and death). Later, after encountering the teachings of Gurdjieff and reading the Vedas and the Upanishads, Daumal abandons these experiments (in particular, the use of drugs, which Gilbert-Lecomte became addicted to) and orients the "work on oneself" in an always more spiritual direction. It is a matter of freeing oneself from the limited number of intellectual and sentimental "postures" in which we are imprisoned in an attempt to access a veritable transformation of the self. Two years before his death, Daumal writes:

> I now better understand what cabbalists and Hasidim say about the "sparks" (the forces) contained in things, which man has the duty to "save"—that is, to take not for himself, and thus definitively enclose them in a greater prison, but to give them back in the end to the Force of forces. Does recalling oneself not perhaps mean, in a certain sense, feeling oneself in this way *between* the inferior and the superior forces, torn apart between the two, but with the possibility of becoming the transformer of the former into the latter?[2]

Even at the point when he is integrally focused on working on himself, Daumal never abandons writing. At the beginning of the 1940s, he starts to write a sort of tale, in which his spiritual search seems to find its final style: *Mount Analogue*. "I am writing a rather long tale," he announces to a friend,

> in which one will see a group of human beings who have realized they are in prison, who have understood they first of all need to quit this prison (since the tragedy is clinging on to it), and who set off in search of a superior humanity freed from the prison, where they can find the help they need. And they find it, because some friends and I have found the door. Real life begins only at this door. This tale will be structured like an adventure novel and entitled *Mount Analogue*: it is the symbolic mountain that unites Heaven and Earth; a way that must materially and humanly *exist*, since otherwise our situation would be hopeless. Probably some excerpt will be published in the next issue of the journal *Mesures*.[3]

The gap between what is at stake—the door that unites heaven and earth—and the "adventure novel" of which some extracts will be published in a literary journal is blatant. Why does the work on oneself, which has to lead to spiritual liberation, need the work on an opus [*lavoro a un'opera*]? If Mount Analogue materially exists, why give it the shape of a narrative fiction, which was initially presented as a "treatise of psychological mountaineering," and which the author

certainly did not care to include among the master-
pieces of twentieth-century literature? Since Daumal
did not either intend to set his novel on the same level
as what he called the revealed "great Scriptures" (such
as the Gospels and the Upanishads), should we not
rather ask whether, as happens in any literary work,
Mount Analogue only exists *analogously* in the writing
that speaks about it? That is, whether, for some reason,
the work on oneself is only possible in the at least
apparently incongruous form of the writing of a book?

The idea that in working on a work of art, a
transformation of the author is at stake—that is, in
the last resort, a transformation of his life—would
have in all likelihood been incomprehensible for
the ancients. But the classical world knew a place—
Eleusis—in which those who were initiated into the
mysteries attended a sort of theatrical pantomime, the
vision (the *epopsia*) of which transformed them and
made them happier. The catharsis, the purification of
passions that, according to Aristotle, was felt by the
spectators of a tragedy, perhaps contained a weak echo
of the Eleusinian experience. The fact that Euripides
was accused of revealing in his tragedies the mysteries
that had to remain ineffable nonetheless shows that
the ancients considered the putting in strict relation of
the religious transformation of existence and a literary

work to be inappropriate (even if tragic performance was originally part of a cult).

For Daumal, however, working on an opus has a meaning only if it coincides with the edification of the self. This amounts to turning life into the stakes and, at the same time, the touchstone of the opus. For this, he can summarize his supreme belief as an itinerary from death to life:

> I am dead because I have no desire,
> I have no desire because I think I possess,
> I think I possess because I do not try to give.
> Trying to give, one sees one *has* nothing,
> Seeing one has nothing, one tries to give oneself,
> Trying to give oneself, one sees one *is* nothing,
> Seeing one is nothing, one tries to become,
> Desiring to become, one lives.

If the real work is life and not the written work, we should not be surprised that among the precepts for the liberation of the self there are also, like in any esoteric tradition, hygienic prescriptions and suggestions that seem more suitable to a diet than a mystical isagoge: "Relaxing ten or even five minutes in a reclining position before every meal will help you; in particular, it will relax the epigastric region and the throat."[4]

The fact that literary creation can and even must go together with a process of self-transformation, and

that poetic writing has a meaning only to the extent
that it transforms the author into a prophet, was
implicit in the testimony of the poet that *Le Grand Jeu*
indeed elected as its emblem: Arthur Rimbaud. The
fascination that the work he has abruptly bequeathed
us continues to exert over his readers derives precisely
from the twofold dimension of which it seems to
consist and in which it moves. Here it is not important
that asceticism has the form of a "long, immense
et raisonné dérèglement de tous les sens."[5] What is
again decisive is the work on oneself as the only way
to access the literary work and the literary work as
the protocol for the carrying out of an operation
on oneself. Rimbaud's letter to Demeny states
programmatically that "la première étude de l'homme
qui veut être poète est sa propre connaissance, entière;
il cherche son âme, il l'inspecte, il la tente, l'apprend.
Dès qu'il la sait, il doit la cultiver. . . . Je dis qu'il faut
être *voyant*, se faire *voyant*."[6] But precisely for this, the
book that follows—*A Season in Hell*—presents us with
the paradox of a literary work that claims to describe
and verify a non-literary experience, whose place is
the subject who, transforming himself in this way,
becomes capable of writing it. The value of the work
derives from the experiment, but the latter serves only
the writing of the work—or, at least, attests to its value
only by means of it.

The contradiction in which the author has thus found himself is perhaps best conveyed by the lucid diagnosis: "Je devins un opéra fabuleux."[7] An opera, that is, a performance, in which the "simple hallu-cinations" and the "sacred" disorder of his mind are offered to his own disenchanted gaze as if they were staged in a third-rate theater. We are then not sur-prised that, facing this vicious circle, the author very soon became disgusted with both his work and the "deliriums" that it witnessed, and that he abandoned literature and Europe without regrets. According to the (not always credible) testimony of his sister Isa-belle, "il brûla (très gaiement, je vous assure) toutes ses œuvres dont il se moquait et plaisantait."[8]

We are left with the peculiar and tenacious impression that the decision to abandon poetry in order to trade weapons and camels in Abyssinia and Aden is an integral part of his work. In Rimbaud's biography, this extreme annexation of life by work does not, obviously, have any foundation; however, it bears witness to the lasting confusion between art and life that Romanticism has produced (the letter to Demeny, with its opposition between the ancient man who does not work on himself—*ne se travaillant pas*—and the Romantic poets, who become *voyants*, stands as a perspicuous document of Romanticism).

When Rimbaud wrote his letter, Hegel had already long formulated his diagnosis concerning the "death" of art—or, more precisely, concerning the fact that art had left to science the central position in the vital energies of civilized mankind. His diagnosis was actually also applied to the same extent to religion: the image Hegel uses to describe the decline and twilight of art is, in fact, that, facing the beautiful images of Christ and the Holy Virgin, "our knees no longer bend." In Western culture, religion, art, and science seem to constitute three different and inseparable fields that rotate, join forces, and incessantly combat each other, where none of them ever manages to completely eliminate the other two. The man of science, who chased religion and art away from their glorious abodes, witnesses with Romanticism their return in a precarious and unlikely coalition. The artist now has the emaciated face of the mystic and the ascetic; his work assumes a liturgical aura and aspires to be a prayer. When the religious mask loses its credibility, the artist, who has sacrificed his art for a superior truth, shows his real worth: he is only a living body, only a bare life, who presents itself as such and demands inhuman rights.

In any case, what is acknowledged in Rimbaud's decision is the failure of the Romantic attempt at uniting mystical practice and poetry, work on oneself and the production of a work.

The fact that exercising an artistic practice (in the broad sense that the term *ars* has in the Middle Ages, which includes all crafts and professions) cannot support man's happiness and that they are, however, somehow connected is something implicit in the passage from the *Summa contra Gentiles* in which Thomas Aquinas briefly reflects on the matter. "The ultimate happiness [*ultima felicitas*] of man," he states, "cannot amount to the operation of an art [*in operatione artis*]." The end of art is, in fact, the production of artifacts (*artificiata*), and these cannot stand for the end of human life, since, to the extent that they are made for the use of mankind, man is the end of work and not vice versa.

The ultimate happiness of man rather consists in the contemplation of God. Yet insofar as human operations, including those of art, are directed toward the contemplation of God as their own end, there exists a necessary nexus between the operations of art and happiness. "There is needed for the perfection of contemplation soundness of body, to which all the products of art that are necessary for life are directed." The directing of every human operation toward happiness thus guarantees that the works of the arts are themselves somehow inscribed in the contemplative regime, which amounts to the supreme end of mankind.

The outcome of an imprudent juxtaposition of artistic practice and work on oneself is the cancellation of the artistic work. This is evident in the avant-gardes. Here, the primacy accorded to the artist and the creative process takes place, curiously, at the expense of what they were supposed to produce. The most characteristic intention of Dada was not so much an attack directed against art—which is rather transformed into something halfway between mystical discipline and critical operation—as against the artistic work, which was dismissed and derided. In this sense, Hugo Ball, on the threshold of religious conversion, suggested to artists to stop producing works in order to commit themselves to "energetic efforts of reanimation on oneself." As for Duchamp, by producing *The Large Glass* and inventing the *ready-made*, he intended to show that it was possible to go "beyond the physical act of painting," so as to bring artistic activity back to "the service of the spirit." He writes: "Dada was an extreme protest against the physical side of painting. It was a metaphysical attitude." But it is perhaps in Yves Klein that the abolition of the artistic work in the name of artistic activity and of the work on oneself is enunciated most clearly. Klein writes: "My paintings are the ashes of my art," and he pushes the negation of the artistic work to its extreme consequences:

What I am trying to achieve—my future development, my solution to the problem—is to no longer do anything at all, as quickly as possible, but consciously, with care and caution. I only try to be. I will be a "painter." People will say of me: that's the "painter." And I will feel myself to be a "painter," a real one, precisely, because I won't paint. . . . The fact of my existence as a painter will be the most "wonderful" pictorial work of all times.[9]

However, as shown far too evidently by these words, with the abolition of the artistic work, unexpectedly, the work on oneself also disappears. The artist, who has dismissed the artistic work in order to focus on the transformation of the self, is now absolutely unable to produce anything other than an ironic mask, or he simply exhibits his living body without restraint. He is a man who no longer has content, who observes—we do not know whether with pleasure or terror—the void that the disappearance of the work has left inside him.

From here follows the progressive displacement of artistic activity toward politics. Aristotle opposed *poiesis*, the activities of the artisan and the artist, which produce an independent object, to *praxis*, that is, political action, which has its end in itself. In this sense, we can say that avant-gardes, who want to abolish the artistic work at the expense of artistic activity, are doomed, whether they like it or not, to

transfer their workshop from the floor of *poiesis* to that
of *praxis*. This means that they are forced to abolish
themselves and be transformed into a political movement. According to Guy Debord's irrefutable verdict:
"Surrealism wanted to realize art without abolishing
it, and Dadaism wanted to abolish art without realizing it. Situationists want to abolish art and, at the
same time, realize it."

A too-close connection between the literary work
and the work on oneself may take the shape of an
exacerbation of the spiritual search. This is the case
with Cristina Campo. Here the development of the
very original talent of the writer is first guided, but
then progressively eroded and finally devoured, by
an obsessive search for perfection. Perfection is here
formal perfection—as in the "unforgivable" writers
she never tires of commending—and, at the same
time and to the same extent, spiritual perfection,
which almost scornfully marks in the former its
contemptuousness. She almost obsessively repeats
to herself, "Attention is the only path toward the
inexpressible, the only way to mystery," and, in this
way, she forgets her other, more felicitous, obsession:
the fairy tale, before which any demand for spiritual
perfection cannot but stop its claims. A writing
of matchless lightness gets in this way lost in the

impossible task of "clapping with only one hand";
eventually, it is only able to praise the peremptory
beauty of authors who do not need any eulogy. But
even this is not enough for her unabated hunger for
purity: the cult of idolatrized authors is gradually
replaced with the passion for ritual cult in the strict
sense, that is, for liturgy. She is unable to get on top
of her book on *Poetry and Ritual,* which she planned
to write in her final years; but meanwhile, the love for
literature is slowly corroded and cancelled by her new,
unfulfillable, and indubitable love. Her adored Proust
stops talking to her:

> Even the last, solemn page of the great poem, the stone
> that closes on the tomb, the last, majestic word, "le
> Temps," left me inexplicably cold. The Rex tremendae
> maiestatis was perhaps outside my door: he did not do
> anything; he just let the beloved things sound barren as
> if they were made of paper.[10]

As in the abhorred avant-gardes, here, too, the drift
is somehow political: Cristina Campo consecrates the
last part of her life to an equally bitter and merciless
battle against the reformation of liturgy that followed
the Second Vatican Council.

A field in which the work on oneself and the
production of a work are eminently presented as

consubstantial and indivisible is alchemy. The *opus alchymicum* in fact implies that the transformation of metals occurs hand in hand with the transformation of the subject, that the search for and production of the philosopher's stone coincides with the spiritual creation or recreation of the subject that carries it out. On the one hand, alchemists expressly affirm that their work is a material operation that results in the transmutation of metals, which, going through a series of phases or stages (named after the colors they assume—*nigredo*, *albedo*, *citrinitas*, and *rubedo*), reach perfection in gold as their outcome. On the other hand, they reiterate in an equally persistent way that the metals of which they speak are not the usual metals, that the philosophical gold is not the *aurum vulgi*, vulgar gold, and that in the end the initiated becomes himself the philosophical stone ("Transmute yourselves from dead stones into living philosophical stones").

The title of one of the oldest alchemical works, traditionally attributed to Democritus, *Physikà kai Mystikà*, paradigmatically expresses this interpenetration of the two levels of the "great work," which adepts have always stated should be understood *tam ethice quam physice*, that is, in an equally moral and material sense. For this, rather than those historians of science such as Berthelot and Von Lippmann, who considered alchemy simply as an anticipation, although obscure and embryonic, of modern chemistry, or the esoterics such as Evola and Fulcanelli, who saw in alchemical texts nothing other than the codified transcription of an experience of initiation, it was scholars such as Eliade and Jung, who stressed the indivisibility of the two aspects of the *opus*, who were more successful. For Eliade, alchemy presents itself as the projection onto matter of a mystical experience. Although it is doubtless the case that alchemical operations were real operations on metals, "alchemists projected onto matter the initiatory function of suffering. . . . In his laboratory, the alchemist operated on himself, on his psycho-physical life as well as on his moral and spiritual experience." Just as the matter of metals dies and is regenerated, so, too, does the soul of the alchemist perish and is born again, and the production of gold coincides with the resurrection of the adept.

Whether they focus on chemical practice or highlight the spiritual itinerary, studies on alchemy have in common an insufficient attention to the text of alchemical treatises and compilations, which constitute our only source on the topic. They amount to an endless *corpus*; whoever wants today to approach the knowledge of the "Great Work" cannot avoid consulting them, be they the Greek

alchemical manuscripts edited by Berthelot, the
octavo volumes of the *Theathrum Chemicum*, or
those of the *Bibliotheca chemica curiosa* and of the
Museum Hermeticum, in which are collected in
vast anthologies, thanks to the compiling fervor of
seventeenth-century scholars, the teachings of the
"philosophers." The reader who browses through
these texts cannot but have the impression of facing
a singular "literature," whose content and forms
are rigidly codified with a monotony and a false
modesty that rival literary genres renowned for their
incomparable unreadability—such as certain medieval
allegorical poems or contemporary pornographic
novels. The "characters" (a king or a queen, who are
also the sun and the moon, the male and the female,
or sulfur and mercury), as in all novels worthy of this
name, go through all kinds of vicissitudes, officiate
at weddings and have sex, give birth, encounter
dragons and eagles, die (the terrifying experience of
the *nigredo*, the black work) and joyfully resurrect.
The plot, however, remains incomprehensible until
the end, since to the very extent that authors describe
its episodes, the narration—already enigmatic and
chaotic—seems to incessantly allude to an extra-
textual practice, and we do not understand whether
it has to take place in a furnace or in the soul of the
alchemist or of his reader. The impression of obscurity

is often enhanced by the images that brighten the manuscripts or illustrate the printed books; these are also so fascinating and allusive that the reader can hardly detach himself from them.

The *lectio facilior*[11] is that this is simply a cryptographic writing, which can be read only by those who have its cipher. But in addition to the fact that one would then not understand the unheard of proliferation of this literature, a passage from the influential treatise *Liber de magni lapidis compositione* seems to exclude it without reservation, claiming that alchemical books are not written to transmit science but only to encourage philosophers to look for it.

But even in this case, why writing? Why do we have this unexplainable and overwhelming proliferation of texts that actually have nothing to communicate?

The *opus alchymicum*'s attempt to make the work on oneself coincide perfectly with the production of a work leaves us with a remainder that is both embarrassing and irremovable: an immense, pompous, and all in all boring alchemical literature. Yet in the insidious *no-man's-land* of alchemy as a historical phenomenon, this literature is our only certainty and point of reference. What seemed to be legitimized only as a document of an external practice acquires in this way an unexpected

autonomous legitimization. Nothing attests to the
self-sufficiency of the alchemical text better than its
specious and non-documentable reference to what
is beyond it. In this sense, alchemical literature is
the place where, perhaps for the first time, a writing
has tried to found its absoluteness by means of a
reference—both fictitious and real in an undecidable
manner—to an extra-textual practice. From here
follows the attraction that alchemy has exerted on
those writers, from Rimbaud to Cristina Campo,
who have obstinately attempted to keep the two
practices united: what they were seeking was,
literally, an *alchimie du verbe,* which looked for
salvation in the transmutation of speech and for
the transfiguration of language in salvation. The
work (or the non-work) of Raymond Roussel—
where the alchemy of language becomes a rebus—is
the emblem—both fascinating and inane, and
fascinating precisely because of its inanity—in
which this attempt exhibits its own impasse almost
heraldically.

In the author who inspired Cristina Campo, Simone
Weil, the distinction between work on oneself and
on an external work is expressed crudely through the
image of the emission of semen inside the body rather
than outside it:

The Ancients believed that during childhood the semen circulates, mingled with the blood throughout the whole body. . . . The belief that with the man that is non-attached the semen once again circulates through-out the whole body . . . is certainly bound up with the conception of the state of childhood as being identical with that state of immortality which is the gateway to salvation. Instead of being emitted outside the body, the semen is emitted within the body itself; just as creative potentiality, of which it is at once the image and, in a sense, the physiological basis, is emitted not outside the soul, but within the soul itself in the case of anyone who is oriented towards absolute good. . . . Man, by emit-ting his semen within himself, begets himself. Here we certainly have the image and no doubt effectively, in a certain manner of speaking, the physiological condition of a spiritual process.[12]

As in alchemy, the spiritual process that is here in question coincides with its own regeneration. But what is a creation that never exits itself? How is it different from what Freudianism (of which Simone Weil once wrote that it "would be absolutely true if the concep-tion behind it were not oriented in such a manner as to make it absolutely false")[13] calls narcissism, that is, the introjection of the libido? The child, who is here taken as a model of "an orientation not oriented towards something," does not simply refrain from any operation directed outside himself; rather, he config-ures this operation in a particular way, which we call a game, for which the production of an external object is certainly not the main purpose. To use Weil's image, the semen, the genetic principle, here incessantly exits and reenters the agent, and the external work is created and equally de-created in an incessant manner. The child works on himself only to the extent that he works outside himself—and this is precisely the definition of a game.

The idea that in every reality—and in every text—one should distinguish an appearance from a hidden meaning, which the initiated needs to know, lies at the basis of esotericism. An esoteric of the twentieth century, who was also a scholar of the Shia tradition, summarized it in the following way:

> All that is exterior, every appearance, every exotericism [*zahir*], has a reality that is internal, hidden, esoteric [*batin*]. The exoteric is the apparent form, the epiphanic place [*mazhar*] of the esoteric. It is therefore reciprocally necessary that there is an exoteric for each esoteric; the former is the visible and manifest aspect of the latter; the esoteric is the real idea [*haqiqat*], the secret, the gnosis, the meaning, and the supersensible [*ma'ana*] content of the exoteric. The one has subsistence and consistency in the visible world; the other in the supersensible world [*'alam al-ghayb*].[14]

The meaning of the Shia doctrine of the hidden Imam is the application of esotericism to history: the material history of facts is punctually matched by a hierohistory, founded on the occultation of the twelfth Imam. The Imam is in fact hidden because men have made themselves unable to know him, and the initiated are those in whom the esoteric meaning of historical events is fully revealed.

If we define mystery as what needs a shell, it is evident that what esotericism sins against is precisely the mystery that it would like to safeguard. That is to say, the esoteric sins twice: the first time against what is hidden, which when unveiled is no longer such, and the second time against the veil, because when it is lifted it loses its raison d'être. This can also be expressed by saying that the esoteric sins against beauty, because the lifted veil is no longer beautiful and the unveiled meaning loses its form. A corollary to this principle is that no artist can be an esoteric, and, reciprocally, no esoteric can be an artist.

At this stage we understand Cristina Campo's passionate, tenacious, and contradictory insistence on liturgy as a supreme form of poetry. For her, what is at stake is nothing less than saving beauty—on condition, however, of holding to the fact that beauty—which she calls liturgy—is, according to the proper meaning of the Greek term *mysterion*, a sacred drama, whose form cannot be altered, since it neither reveals nor represents, but simply presents something. *It is not*

liturgy as beauty

the invisible that it makes visible but the visible. If, on the other hand, we understand beauty, as is usually the case and as at times Cristina Campo herself seems to believe, as a visible symbol of a hidden meaning, it then loses its mystery and, for this, also its beauty.

During the last years of his life, Michel Foucault focused his research more and more on a theme that he enunciated several times with the formula "the care of the self." For him it was primarily a matter of investigating the practices and the apparatuses—examination of conscience, *hypomnemata*, ascetic exercises—to which the twilight of Antiquity entrusted one of its most tenacious intentions: no longer knowledge but the government of the self and the work on oneself (*epimeleia heautou*). Yet there was also a more ancient theme at stake in this investigation, namely, that of the constitution of the subject and, in particular, "the way in which the individual constitutes himself as the moral subject of his own actions." These two themes merged into a third, which Foucault evoked several times in his last interviews without really tackling it as such: the idea of an "aesthetics of existence," of the self and of life understood as a work of art.

Pierre Hadot has for this reason reproached Foucault for thinking the "work of the self on the self"

and the "exercise of the self" that were typical of
ancient philosophy only in aesthetic terms, as if the
task of the philosopher could be compared to that
of an artist dedicated to shaping his life as a work
of art, while this should rather be an "overcoming"
of the self, not its "construction." The accusation is
unfounded since an examination of the passages in
which Foucault evokes this theme shows that he never
locates it in an aesthetic context but always in that of
an ethical search. Already in the first lecture of the
1981–82 course *The Hermeneutics of the Subject*, as if
he anticipated Hadot's objection, Foucault warns us
against the modern temptation to read phrases such
as "care of the self" or "looking after oneself" in an
aesthetic rather than moral sense: "Now you are well
aware that there is a certain tradition (or rather several
traditions) that dissuades us (us, now, today) from
giving any positive value to these formulations . . . and
above all from making them the basis of a morality.
[They] sound to our ears rather like—what? Like a
sort of challenge and defiance, a desire for radical ethical change, a sort of moral dandyism, the assertion-
challenge of a fixed aesthetic and individual stage."[15]
Against these so to speak aestheticizing interpretations
of the care of the self, Foucault specifies shortly after
that precisely "this injunction to 'take care of oneself'
is the basis for the constitution of what have without

doubt been the most austere, strict, and restrictive moralities known in the West."

In the introduction to the second volume of *History of Sexuality*, the pertinence of the "aesthetics of existence" to the ethical sphere is clarified beyond doubt. The "arts of existence" the book deals with and the techniques of the self through which men have tried to turn their life into "an oeuvre that carries certain aesthetic values and meets certain stylistic criteria" are actually "voluntary and reasoned practices" through which men establish for themselves behavioral canons that carry out a function which Foucault unreservedly defines as "etho-poietic."[16] In an interview published one year before his death, he specifies that the care of the self is not for the Greeks an aesthetic problem and was "considered itself as ethical."[17]

The problem of the care of the self [*cura di sé*] or work on oneself [*lavoro su di sé*] contains a preliminary difficulty, of a logical and, prior to that, even grammatical nature. The pronoun *se*, which in Indo-European languages expresses reflexivity, lacks for this reason the nominative case. It presupposes a grammatical subject (which carries out the reflexive action), but this can never be itself in the position of the subject. The self [*sé*], insofar as in this sense it coincides with a reflexive relation, can never be a substance, or a substantive. And if, as Bréal has shown, the term *ethos* is nothing other than the pronominal root of the Greek reflexive *e* followed by the suffix *-thos*, and therefore means, simply and literally, "seity" [*seità*], that is, the way in which each of us experiences oneself, this entails that the idea of an ethical subject is a contradiction in terms. From here follow the aporias and difficulties that, as seen, threaten every attempt to work on oneself; the subject who wants to enter into a relation with oneself sinks into a dark and bottomless abyss—where only a God can save him. The *nigredo*, the obscure night implicit in every search for the self, has its roots here.

Foucault seems to be aware of this contradiction when he writes that "the self with which one has the relationship is nothing other than the relationship itself. . . . It is in short the immanence, or better, the ontological adequacy of the self to the relationship."[18] In other words, there is no subject prior to the relationship with the self: the subject is this relationship and not one of its terms. It is in this perspective—for which the work of the self on the self is presented as an aporetic task—that Foucault refers to the idea of the self and of life as a work of art. In an interview with Dreyfus and Rabinow, he says that "there is only one practical consequence of the idea that the subject is not given in advance: we have to create ourselves

life as
work
of art →

as a work of art. . . . We should not have to refer the creative activity of somebody to the kind of relation he has to himself, but should relate the kind of relation one has to oneself to a creative activity."[19]

How should we understand this last claim? It can certainly mean that, from the moment the subject is not given in advance, it is necessary to construct it like the artist constructs his work of art. But it is equally legitimate to read it in the sense that the relation-ship with oneself and the work on oneself become possible only if they are linked with a creative activ-ity. Foucault seems to suggest something similar in a 1968 interview with Claude Bonnefoy that focuses on the creative activity Foucault practiced, namely, writing. After stating that he feels obliged to write because writing gives rise to a sort of absolution, which is indispensable for happiness, he specifies: "It's not the writing that's happy, it's the joy of existing that's attached to writing, which is slightly different."[20] Happiness—the ethical task par excellence, at which every work on oneself aims—is "attached" to writing, that is, becomes possible only through a creative prac-tice. The care of the self necessarily passes through an *opus*; it inextricably implies an alchemy.

Paul Klee exemplifies a perfect coincidence between work on oneself and artistic practice. None of Klee's works is simply a work: they all somehow refer to something else, which is not, however, their author but rather his transformation and regeneration in another place, in a

> Land without ties, new land
> With no warm breath of memory,
> . . . Reinless!
> Where no mother's womb carried me.

The coincidence between the two levels, between the creation of works and the recreation of the author, is here so perfect that, contemplating Klee's paintings, we do not really ask how the work on the opus and the work on oneself have found unity, but rather how we could even envisage their separation. The one who is recreated is in fact not the author registered at birth but, to quote the epitaph one can read on the painter's gravestone in Berne's cemetery, a being whose abode is "just as much with the dead as with the unborn" and who is, for this, "closer than usual to creation."

It is in creation, in the "point of genesis," and not in the work, that creation and recreation (or de-creation, as one should say) perfectly coincide. In Klee's lectures and notes the idea that what is essential is "not form, but formation [*Gestaltung*]" appears again and again. We should never "let go of the reins of formation, and cease creative work." And just as creation continuously recreates the author, relieving him of his identity, so, too, does recreation prevent the work from being simply a form and not a formation. As Klee writes in a 1922 note, "Creation lives as a genesis beneath the visible surface of the work": potentiality, the creative principle is never exhausted by the actual work, but continues to live in it, and rather is "what is essential in the work." For this, the creator can coincide with the work, find in it his only abode and his only happiness: "A painting does not have specific ends; its only aim is to make us happy."

In what way can the relation with a creative practice (an art, in the broad sense this word had in the Middle Ages) make possible the relation with oneself and the work on oneself? What is at stake is not only the—certainly important—fact that this practice provides a mediation and a plane of consistency to the otherwise elusive relation with oneself. Here— like in the *opus alchymicum*—the risk would, then, be that of delegating to an external practice—the transformation of metals into gold, the production of a work—the operation on oneself, while between the two there is actually nothing other than an analogical or metaphorical passage.

It is therefore necessary that—through the relation with the work on oneself—the creative practice

itself undergo a transformation. The relation with an
external practice (the opus) makes possible the work
on oneself only to the extent that it is constituted as a
relation to a potentiality. A subject who tried to define
and shape himself only through his own opus would
be doomed to incessantly exchanging his life and
reality with his own opus. The real alchemist is rather
the one who—in the opus and through the opus—
contemplates only the potentiality that produced it.
For this, Rimbaud called "vision" the transformation
of the poetic subject he had tried to reach by all possible means. What the poet, who has become a "seer,"
contemplates is language—that is, not the written
opus but the potentiality of writing. And given that, in
Spinoza's words, potentiality is nothing other than the
essence or nature of every being, inasmuch as it has
the capacity of doing something, contemplating this
potentiality is also the only possible access to the *ethos*
and the "seity."

Certainly, the contemplation of a potentiality can
only be given in an opus; but, in contemplation, the
opus is deactivated and made inoperative and, in this
way, given back to possibility, opened to a new possible
use. A truly poetic form of life is the one that contemplates in its opus its own potentiality to do and not to
do, and finds peace in it. A living being can never be
defined by its opus but only by its inoperativity, that

is, by the way in which, maintaining itself, in an opus, in relation with pure potentiality, it constitutes itself as form-of-life, in which what is at stake is no longer either life or opus but happiness. The form-of-life is the point in which the work on an opus and the work on oneself perfectly coincide. The painter, the poet, the thinker—and, in general, anyone who practices an "art" or an "activity"—are not the appointed sovereign subjects of a creative operation and of an opus; they are rather anonymous living beings who, contemplating and making at each turn inoperative the opus of language, of vision, and of bodies, try to experience themselves and keep in relation with a potentiality, that is, to constitute their life as form-of-life. Only at this point can opus and Great Opus, metallic gold and the gold of the philosophers, be completely identified.

final

Note on the Texts

All texts are unpublished, with the exception of "What Is the Act of Creation?," which reproduces with some changes the text of a lecture given at the Accademia di Architettura of Mendrisio in November 2012—published in a limited edition in Giorgio Agamben, *Archeologia dell'opera* (Mendrisio 2013). "Easter in Egypt" reproduces the text of an intervention at the one-day seminar on the correspondence between Ingeborg Bachmann and Paul Celan, *Troviamo le parole: Lettere, 1948–1973*, held at Villa Sciarra, Rome, at the Istituto italiano di Studi Germanici, in June 2010. "On the Difficulty of Reading" was presented at the round table *Leggere è un rischio* during the Fiera della piccola e media editoria of Rome, in December 2012. "From the Book to the Screen" is the modified version of a lecture given at the Fondazione Cini of Venice in January 2010.

Notes

The Fire and the Tale

1. Gershom Scholem, *Major Trends in Jewish Mysticism* (New York: Schocken Books, 1961), 349–50. [Where necessary, citations are adapted to Agamben's own citations in Italian. Source citations are provided only when they are provided by the author.—Trans.]

2. The Italian *storia* means both "history" and "story," in the sense of "tale."—-Trans.

3. Gershom Scholem, *Briefe* (Munich: Beck, 1994), 1:471ff.

Mysterium Burocratium

1. As if God did not exist / were not given.—Trans.

Parable and Kingdom

1. Eberhard Jüngel, *Paulus und Jesus* (Tübingen: Mohr Siebeck, 2004), 135.

2. Saint Gregory of Nazianzus, comp., *The Philocalia of Origen*, translated by George Lewis (Edinburgh: T. & T. Clark, 1911), 2.3.

3. Ibid., 2.1.

4. Origen, *Commentary on Matthew*, in *Ante-Nicene Fathers*, vol. 9 (Buffalo, NY: Christian Literature Publishing, 1896), 10,14.

What Is the Act of Creation?

1. In line with most translations of Agamben's works, I have rendered the Italian *potenza* as "potentiality" when it refers to Aristotle's notion of *dynamis* (Adam Kotsko opts for "potential" in the recent *The Use of Bodies*, a book with which *The Fire and the Tale* shares many themes). In *The Kingdom and the Glory*, I translated *potenza* as "power," specifying the Italian original in brackets. Normally, both *potenza* and *potere* would be translated as "power" in English. While the distinction between *potenza* and *potere* is by all means crucial for Agamben, and must be taken into account in translation, "potentiality" and "potential" do not fully exhaust the meaning of *potenza*. The reader might also bear in mind that *dynamis* is often rendered in English as "potency," which is perhaps closer to *potenza* than "potentiality" and "potential."—Trans.

2. In the interest of consistency with previous translations, I have rendered *impotenza* as "impotentiality." Although, for Agamben, *impotenza* does not imply inability, impossibility, or passivity, the reader should be reminded that it primarily means "impotence."—Trans.

3. *Acquiescentia in se ipso* is usually rendered in English translations of Spinoza's *Ethics* as "self-esteem" or "self-satisfaction."—Trans.

Easter in Egypt

1. Ingeborg Bachmann and Paul Celan, *Correspondence* (London: Seagull, 2010), 257.

2. See Celan's letter to Bachmann dated Oct. 31, 1957.

From the Book to the Screen

1. James Lord, *A Giacometti Portrait* (New York: Farrar, Strauss and Giroux, 1980).

2. Italo Calvino to Giorgio Manganelli, March 7, 1969, now in-

cluded in Giorgio Manganelli, *Nuovo commento* (Milan: Adelphi, 1993), 149–50.

Opus Alchymicum

1. René Daumal, *Il lavoro su di sé: Lettere a Geneviève e Louis Lief,* edited by C. Rugafiori (Milan: Adelphi, 1998), 118.

2. Ibid., 121.

3. René Daumal, *La conoscenza di sé*, edited by C. Rugafiori (Milan: Adelphi, 1972), 177.

4. Daumal, *Il lavoro su di sé*, 77.

5. A "long, immense and reasoned imbalance of all senses."—Trans.

6. "The first study of a man who wants to become a poet is his own understanding, complete; he seeks his soul, inspects it, tests it, learns it. As soon as he knows it, he must cultivate it. . . . I say that one must be a *seer*, make oneself a *seer*."—Trans.

7. "I became a fabulous opera."—Trans.

8. "He burnt (with gusto, I can assure you) all his works, of which he made fun."—Trans.

9. Yves Klein, *Le dépassement de la problématique de l'art et autres écrits* (Paris: École Nationale Supérieure des Beaux-Arts, 2003), 236.

10. Cristina De Stefano, *Belinda e il mostro: Vita segreta di Cristina Campo* (Milan: Adelphi, 2002), 180.

11. The easiest reading, or interpretation.—Trans.

12. Simone Weil, *The Notebooks of Simone Weil*, trans. Arthur Mills (New York: Routledge, 2004), 470–71.

13. Ibid., 471–72.

14. Henry Corbin, *L'Imam nascosto* (Milan: SE, 2008), 21–22.

15. Michel Foucault, *The Hermeneutics of the Subject* (New York: Palgrave Macmillan, 2005), 12.

16. Michel Foucault, *The Use of Pleasure*, vol. 2 of *The History of Sexuality* (New York: Vintage, 1990), 13.

17. "The Ethic of Care for the Self as a Practice of Freedom: An Interview with Michel Foucault on January 20, 1984," *Philosophy and Social Criticism* 12 (July 1987): 115.

18. Foucault, *The Hermeneutics of the Subject*, 533.

19. Michel Foucault, "On the Genealogy of Ethics: An Overview of Work in Progress," in *The Foucault Reader*, edited by Paul Rabinow (London: Penguin, 1991), 351.

20. Michel Foucault, *Speech Begins After Death* (Minneapolis: University of Minnesota Press, 2013), 64.

MERIDIAN

Crossing Aesthetics